FOREX AND SWING TRADING FOR BEGINNERS

Learn FOREX AND Swing Trading and crush
the Market today.

a Quick GUIDE for Beginners

to create Passive Income and Make Money With

Financial Leverage and Risk Management. ©

Introduction Forex Trading

Although we cannot say that currency trading is as old as currency, it is probably pretty close. It will be difficult for most people in the Western world to imagine, but there was a time when currency was not commonplace. Indeed, even in the 20th century, there were still parts of the world where trade took place primarily by barter, the direct exchange of one commodity for another. Currency trading itself can be thought of as a type of barter. Indeed, though the most common form of currency trading is a spot transaction in which there is a trade of a certain amount of one currency for a certain amount of another currency, there are other forms of currency trading that perhaps are more obviously a type of barter. Even in Ancient Egypt, the oldest major civilization for which we have detailed records and archaeological evidence, exchange was almost entirely in the form of barter. There are records of using iron ingots as a form of currency at this period and, in fact, this form of metal ingot currency was the first real currency that we know of before coinage began to appear in the 6th century B.C. Greek myths (and historical records) tell us of kings like Midas and Croesus who were legendary for their wealth, and though the mythological Midas was most likely legendary, Croesus was an actual historical figure. He ruled the region of Lydia in western Anatolia and his kingdom was the first to utilize modern coinage, which the Greeks rapidly adopted.

One of Croesus's coins still exists in the British Museum, a gold coin from the mid-6th century B.C. The first Lydian coins actually pre-date this and were made of electrum, which is a yellow-colored alloy of gold and silver that was common in the mines of central and western Anatolia, in modern-day Turkey. The earliest Greek coins resembled these first Lydian specimens, and the rapid adoption of coinage throughout the Mediterranean region facilitated trade and the accumulation of wealth by the merchant class. Studying coinage in these early years is interesting because the large number of Greek city-states and other political units in the region has led to a great number of diverse artifacts remaining for us to study. They all served the same purpose: as a means of exchange. Currency was primarily in the form of coinage in the Western world until the 19th century, when paper currency—most often in the form of banknotes—began to appear. In fact, coinage was not the only form of currency before this period, though people often picture a coin with the image of a monarch or deity on its face when they think of currency. In some parts of the world, shells or, again, ingots, were used instead of coins. Of course, money-changing as a pursuit would have begun not long after currency became common, as all it would have required was two currencies to exchange. Various advancements that have occurred since this time have made currency trading the enormous industry it is today, namely the global system that has made essentially all economies on Earth accessible to one another, and the coming of the Digital Age. The single most significant factor in establishing the currency trading industry as a world market was perhaps the internet, though other factors helped along the way.

How Forex Trading Works

Forex trading is not a trade that one can pull off without breaking a sweat before exchanging currencies. There has to be prior preparation, studies done and analyzation of the market patterns to make the first trade. Below is discussed the steps that a trader has to make so as to start trading forexes and be successful while doing so.

Forex Trading Terminology

There are a lot of terms used that are new to a trader who is just starting off and are vocabularies to them. It would do well to an aspiring trader to acquaint themselves with the new terms and understand the meaning behind them and how to use them appropriately when trading. This will prove essential to avoid miscomprehension of certain concepts when trading. To new traders, the terms may be a little bit difficult and also have a completely different meaning than the expected one from its word-formation. The following words discussed below are some of the new vocabularies that will be encountered by a new trader, which are common in the language of trading.

A pip. A pip is the lowest measure of the value of movement of currency under observation. The term pip is, however, an abbreviation of the term-percentage in point. A pip, as the lowest measurable value of the movement that the currency makes, always measures ad 1% of the currency that a trader wants to exchange. When in the forex market a currency increases or decreases by a single pip, the inference has the meaning that the currency either increased or decreased by 1%. A great example is when the market analysis tools show that the US dollar has increased by a pip. This is to mean that the US dollar has increased in its value by $0.0001.

That is how a pip is inferred and it's meaning. Trade is always made in terms of pips, and a trader can make trades with many pips as possible. This is because the pips are the lowest value that is measured by the currency.

The base currency. The base currency is the type of currency that a trader has and is currently holding. The base currency is likely the currency of the country that you're from. If a trader is from the US, his or her base currency will be the US dollar. If the trader is from the UK, the base currency of the trader will be the pound. The base currencies of traders therefore different across many traders around the globe due to different geographical differences.

The asking price. The asking price is a term that is used to refer to the amount of money that your broker firm will demand from or will ask from you when you are making a trade. A broker always demands this price, or this amount of money when they are accepting the pair of currencies to be traded from you. The price id for buying the quote that you've made of the pair of currencies. A note to be made is that the asking price; made by the brokerage firms, is always higher than the bid price, as will be discussed immediately below.

Bid price. The bid price is mostly used in reference to the brokerage firms, where it is the amount of money that the brokers will be willing to buy or to bid the base currency that you are currently holding. The broker firm sets the bid price according to their ability to bid on the base currency that has.

Quote currency. The quote currency, unlike the base currency, is the currency that a trader wants and is willing to purchase, in exchange for his or her base currency. If a trader wants to exchange US dollars to get South African Rand, the currency of South Africa; the Rand is the quote currency. It is always stroked against the base currency when trading and when the currencies are made into pairs.

The spread. This is the commission that the broker firm receives from being a platform where forex trading can take place. When referred to, the spread means the difference in value between the bid price made by the broker and the asking price, also quoted by the broker. **Finding the Right Broker Firm So as to trade forex, you will have to have a brokerage firm that will be an online platform from which you'll open and close trade.** Finding the right broker firm is an important process for other brokers can be a sham out to cheat people of their money. It is therefore paramount that a trader carries out research on the available broker firms and picks out the best and one that is highly recommended for its services. When deciding on which broker firm to go with, look at the ask and the bid price that the broker quotes, and other important aspects including the margin and the leverage level that they offer.

The customer service should also be top-notch for the broker, which will be great for a trader who is just starting off. Most of the broker companies also offer studies on how to carry out forex trading and those come in handy to the new traders. Reviews by other forex traders is a great place to start on choosing the quality of a broker.

Making an Analysis of the Worldwide Economy To make gains and profits and gains in trades that you are going to make, analyzing the economic trends of the worldwide economy is of great import to be fully aware of the factors that may trigger the currencies to increase or decrease in value. **This is important in making a correct prediction on the pair of currencies you're exchanging, whether they will make a profit or a loss.** Factors that are important to look into when evaluating the global economy are like the political climate of countries whose currencies have a strong value, natural factors that may influence the economy of countries, the Gross Domestic Product of the country whose currency you want to exchange with your base currency, and other minor factors such as the investment rate of the said country. Evaluating which countries are looking up to growth and development opportunities is also important in determining the quote currency to use impairing up currencies to make a trade. Also on the analysis of the worldwide economy, when the currency of the country you seek to purchase in exchange of your base currency is doing well and is set to increase in its value, convert your base currency into the quote currency.

On the other hand, convert the quote currency into the base currency in case its value increases. There are various online sites that have analysis tools on the economic performance of different countries that you may seek for them to be your quote currency. Others rank counties in terms of their GDP that makes it easier for you to choose the countries that are projected for growth and development. Being in touch with the trending news globally is a plus in getting information relevant to trading forex. A new forex trader may subscribe to a few forex trading channels and outlets to be constantly on toes of events and happenings that may trigger the value of currencies to either increase o decrease, which may result in the reversal of the outlook of the trade made. Having relevant information at all times is key in making gains and preventing the loss of your money and probably your account is cleared.

Opening the First Trade Pairing currencies and making the first trade; opening and closing a trade happens when the quote currency to be paired by the base currency have been paired and there is an opportune trading window. Opening a trade is making an order to purchase a certain currency and in exchange for your base current through your broker firm. You'll have the analysis tools, that are commonly offered by the brokers in software programs. The execution of making an order in some platforms might be instant while in some other platforms, it might be a tad bit slower. Nonetheless, most brokerage firms offer live prices and values of the currencies that are to traded and their exchange rates and the instant changes to their values are displayed.

The first trade for a new trader might just be one or others might open up new trades over a short period of time. It is advisable that just several enough trades be opened, which the new trader is comfortable and at ease in trading.

Principle Currencies

US Dollar (USD)

To this day, the United States dollar remains the world's most important currency. This is particularly true in Forex. The strength of the US dollar has proven itself to be formidable, despite having gone through a lot of financial roadblocks instigated by local and global turmoil. The strength of the currency can be attributed to the country's continued economic strength. The United States has the largest economy, and the country does possess an abundant and liquid capital. Aside from its economy, the strength of the country's currency can also be attributed to its role in the global stage and might of its political and military presence.

The movements of all other currencies still pivot around the market's perception of the US dollar, making it the fulcrum of the Forex market. The US dollar is the most liquid amongst the other currencies, making it the only option to become the world's reserve currency. Around 65 percent of the world's reserves are in US dollars. Due to this fact, central banks around the world now choose to hold a massive amount of this particular currency within their ledgers.

Investors and businesses also regard the US dollar as the go-to safe currency. This has been proven during different global financial situations. During the global credit crisis in 2009, which caused the Lehman Brothers and Bear Stearns to go bankrupt, the US dollar actually appreciated in value.

Investors who were fearful for the worst moved their assets to US government securities, which resulted in the currency's value increase.

Euro (EUR)

The euro has also much appreciated in value by more than 70 percent since 2002. Investors and traders who bet big on its rise certainly made a lot of profit during that time. Over the years, a lot of confidence has also been put on the currency, making it a good alternative. Similar to other currencies, the euro has had its own share of ups and downs, particularly during the global credit crisis in 2008. The euro peaked at US$1.60 during that year. The global credit crisis wreaked havoc on the European banking system. The situation got worse, and the European Central Bank had to intervene. Several members of the European Union were on the verge of bankruptcy. Portugal, Ireland, Greece, and Spain all received financial support from the IMF and the European Union to avoid defaulting on their debt.

Japanese Yen (JPY)

The Japanese yen has been one of the most successful stories in modern foreign exchange. Japan's recovery after World War II saw it emerge as a formidable economic force on the world stage. Since the yen's introduction to the work market, it has grown by a staggering 400 percent against the US dollar. The rise started with the initial economic boom in Japan and is continuing up to this day. Japan is currently one of the world's second-largest economies, and it was holding that position until China overtook it.

The growth of the Japanese yen has unfortunately halted by the early 1990s. However, it has managed to stay at the same relative value. Price inflation in the country has not been a problem in the country, partly thanks to its sophisticated financial system. Japan currently has one of the largest debts in work, on a per-capita basis, but it continues to enjoy healthy demand for its currency. The country continues to attract large investments from all over the world. The performance of the Japanese yen and the country itself is quite impressive given that it does not have a lot of natural resources. The country mostly gets its commodities and energy needs from other nations.

In the last decade, the value of the yen had slightly declined. This was mainly caused by extremely low-interest rates in Japan, which some investors had taken full advantage of by taken out loans and making investments abroad. The decline was halted when investors decided to let go of their short bets on the currency.

British Pound (GBP)

The British pound, or the pound sterling, is currently the fourth-most-traded currency. Prior to the rise of the US Dollar, it was the strongest currency in the world. The strength of the British pound can be attributed to the fact that London remains to be the preeminent currency trading center in the world. Post-World War II, the British pound had gone through quite the fluctuations. Most of the dips can be attributed to the country's continually rising inflation and unemployment levels.

The country's housing market is also nowhere near as robust as other countries. The United Kingdom's debt is also quite substantial, and its decision to print more money only made it worse.

Swiss Franc (CHF)

The economy's stability is mostly thanks to the country's trade surplus and its profitable exports. This includes the export of highly-valuable jewelry such as expensive Swiss watches, tobacco products, chemicals, and manufacturing equipment. Switzerland also mostly evaded the effects of the global credit crisis thanks to the Swiss National Bank's decision to refrain from printing money.

Similar to the US dollar, the Swiss franc is a safe-haven currency. Some would even argue that it performs better than the US dollar in this regard. In fact, during times of global financial uncertainty, the value of the Swiss franc typically increases more than the other "safe" currencies. As for its movement in the Forex market, the Swiss franc closely mirrors the movement of the euro. This is mostly due to the close relationship with the Swiss and the Eurozone economies. However, the currency's value does deviate in times of political strife, thanks mainly to the country's neutrality in global political issues.

Australian Dollar (AUD)

While it might not sound correct, the Australian dollar is actually one of the strongest commodity currencies in the market. Its movement is closely tied to the movement of global commodity prices. This is mainly since the country is one of the world's largest producers of iron ore, coal, and other precious metals. The country's economy has so far taken advantage of China's growing demand for energy and basic commodities. Thanks to this, the country's economy was really damaged by the recent global financial crisis. Due to its close trade relationship with Asian countries, especially China, the Australian dollar's movement does somewhat mirror that of the Chinese yuan. In fact, some investors even treat the currency as a good proxy for the Chinese yuan.

Canadian Dollar (CAD)

The Canadian dollar is another commodity currency that is closely related to global commodity prices. The country is a large producer of energy commodities such as petroleum, timber, and coal. It also exports a number of agricultural products to different parts of the world. The Canadian dollar took advantage of the commodities boom in the mid-2000s and gained in 2010 where its value equaled that of the US dollar. This was the very first time that the Canadian dollar reached parity with the US dollar in over 30 years. Canada's economy is greatly dependent on that of the United States.

Canada produces oil, electricity, and natural gas for the United States, which purchases around 75 percent of what the country produces. When the United States experiences a downtrend in its economy, the Canadian dollar swiftly follows.

Other Currencies

There are currently around 180 legal currencies that are circulating throughout the world. Amongst those currencies, only a handful are actively traded on the Forex market. Most Forex brokers trade between 40 to 70 currency pairs, with some trading more than others. Aside from the currencies mentioned above, there are a few currencies that have become recently significant. This includes the New Zealand dollar, which is closely influenced by the movement of the Australian dollar. The New Zealand dollar is also greatly reliant on the prices of global commodities. The country is a large producer of agricultural products and dairy-based items. The Chinese Yuan has also recently gained prominence, thanks to the rapid growth of the country's economy. It is arguably a currency that investors should look out for given its sudden emergence into the world stage. China has the second largest economy in the world, and it is one of the biggest international traders out there. The Chinese Yuan is pinned to the US dollar. Apart from the major currencies mentioned above and the recent ones that have gained prominence, all of the other currencies are considered to be exotic currencies. These currencies are also sometimes referred to as emerging market currencies; mostly due to their association with their respective country's emerging economies.

These economies tend to have large fluctuations in the market, mostly due to high inflation and significant political and economic changes. In some cases, some of these currencies can rise to unprecedented levels when times are good. However, these are also the currencies that drop the most during times of crisis.

Along with seven other exotic currencies, these emerging currencies account for a combined 9 percent overall trade volume in the Forex market.

Currency Pairs

Similar to company stocks in the stock market, currencies are assigned three-letter abbreviations, set by the International Standards Organization. This greatly simplifies the quoting and trading of these currencies in the world market.

In Forex trading, exotic currencies are generally paired with major currencies. It is doubtful that a non-major currency will be paired with another non-major currency. As an example, it would be challenging to find an exchange that trades the Uruguay Peso and the Iraqi dinar. However, finding an exchange that trades those currencies with the US dollar is relatively easy. Some companies and individuals do exotic trade pairs with another, but their volume merely is just too small for international brokers.

Currency Quotations

The International Organization for Standardization submitted ISO 4217 in 1978. The standard assigned three-letter codes to represent individual currencies to be used in any application for trading, banking, and commerce. It was also agreed upon that the three-letter alphabetic codes for International Standard ISO 4217 would be used in international trading. The list of codes is also frequently updated, as new currencies emerge and older ones are discontinued.

When it comes to Forex trading, currencies always come in pairs. As an example, a trade made with the US dollar versus the euro would look like this (USD/EUR). The US dollar versus the Canadian dollar would look like this (USD/CAD). It goes without saying that a currency can never be traded without itself.

The first currency indicated in the quotation is called the base currency, while the second one is referred to as the counter currency. A numerical value is assigned to the currency pair that may be up to 4 decimal places. The last decimal place is referred to as a "pip." The value assigned to currency pairs is the amount of the counter currency required to buy one unit of the base currency. As an example, if the USD/CAD is quoted at 1.32, it means that it would currently require 1.32 Canadian dollars to buy one single US dollar. On trading platforms, these values would fluctuate in real-time as the value of each currency varies depending on the market.

Exchange Markets

With central banks, retail Forex brokers, commercial corporations, commercial banks, hedge funds, individual investors, and investment management firms participating in the Forex market, it is easy to see why this market is larger than equity and futures markets combined.

Placing a trade in the forex market is quite simple. The basics of Forex Trading are very similar to the mechanics of other financial markets, such as the stock market. Therefore, traders with prior experience in any type of financial market should be able to understand Forex Trading quite quickly.

Basics of the Forex Market

The FX market is a global network of brokers and computers from around the world; therefore, no single market exchange dominates this market. These brokers are also market makers and often post bid and ask prices for currency pairs, which are often different from the most competitive bid in the FX market.

On a more basic level, **the foreign exchange market** consists of two levels, i.e., the over-the-counter market and the interbank market. The OTC market is where individual traders execute trades through brokers and online platforms. The interbank market, on the other hand, is where large banking institutions trade currencies on behalf of clients or for purposes of balance sheet adjustments and hedging.

The backyard trade advertise (Forex, FX, or money showcase) is a global decentralized or over-the-counter (OTC) exhibit for the exchanging of monetary standards. This market decides backyard change charges for each cash. It comprises all parts of purchasing, selling, and buying and selling financial standards at present or decided costs. As far as replacing volume, it is via a lengthy shot the biggest market on the planet, trailed by means of the Credit advertise.

The Foreign Exchange Market is the place the clients and merchants are related with the deal and acquisition of faraway monetary standards. As it were, the financial varieties of a range of countries are bought and is regarded as a remote trade market. The shape of the outside exchange market consists of countrywide banks, commercial enterprise banks, dealers, exporters and shippers, workers, financial specialists, voyagers. These are the foremost gamers of the outdoor market; their role and spot are seemed in the figure beneath. At the base of a pyramid are the actual customers and retailers of the backyard monetary requirements exporters, shippers, vacationer, speculators, and migrants. They are true customers of the economic standards and approach business banks to get it. The business banks are the second most sizable organ of the far-off change showcase. The banks managing in far flung exchange assume a job of "showcase producers", as in the quote every day the backyard trade quotes for buying and selling of the faraway financial standards.

Additionally, they work as clearing houses, in this manner supporting in clearing out the contrast between the pastime for and the stockpile of financial forms. These banks buy the financial varieties from the professionals and offer it to the purchasers.

The 1/3 layer of a pyramid establishes the far-flung trade specialists. These representatives work as a connection between the countrywide financial institution and the business banks and furthermore between the actual purchasers and commercial enterprise banks. They are the sizeable wellspring of market data. These are surely the humans who do not purchase the outdoor money, but instead strike an arrangement between the purchaser and the vender on a fee premise.

The country wide financial institution of any nation is the summit physique in the association of the exchange showcase. They fill in as the loan specialist of the last resort and the caretaker of outside change of the nation. The country wide bank has the capacity to control and manipulate the outdoor trade promote to assure that it works in the equipped design. One of the substantial factors of the country wide financial institution is to counteract the forceful vacillations in the remote alternate showcase, if important, by direct mediation. Mediation through promoting the cash when it is exaggerated and getting it when it will in familiar be underestimated.

Hours of Operation

The FX market is a 24-hour market, from Monday morning to Friday afternoon in Asia and New York, respectively. Essentially, unlike markets such as commodities, bonds, and equities that close for a while, the forex market does not close even at night. However, there are exceptions. Some currencies for emerging markets, for example, close for a short while during the trading day.

The Currency Giants

By far, the US dollar is the biggest player in Forex Trading, making up approximately 85% of all Forex trades. The second most traded currency is the euro, which makes up close to 39% of all currency trades, while the Japanese yen comes in at third place with 19% of all currency trades.

The reason that these figures do not total 100% is that every Forex transaction involves two currencies. Citigroup and JPMorgan Chase and Co. were the biggest participants in the FX market in 2018, according to a study conducted by Greenwich Associates. Actually, these two banks commanded more than 30% of the global Forex market share.

Goldman Sachs, Deutsche Bank, and UBS made up the remaining top five places. According to a settlement and processing group known as CLS, the daily trading volume in January last year was more than $1.8 trillion. This is a testament to just how popular, and massive Forex Trading is around the world.

Origins of the Forex Market

Up until the First World War, countries based their currencies on precious metals like silver and gold. This system, however, collapsed, and the Bretton Woods agreement became the basis of currencies after the Second World War. This agreement led to the creation of three international organizations to oversee economic activities across the world.

These organizations were the General Agreement on Tariffs and Trade, the International Monetary Fund, and the International Bank for Reconstruction and Development. In addition to creating these international organizations, the agreement adopted the US dollar as the peg for international currencies, instead of gold.

In return, the US government had to back up dollar supplies with an equivalent amount or value of gold reserves. This system, however, ended in 1971 when Richard Nixon, the US president at the time, suspended the US dollar's convertibility into gold. Nowadays, currencies can pick their own peg, and the forces of demand and supply determine their value.

Trading Approaches

There are several types of forex strategies; however, it is important to choose the right one based preferred trading style to trade successfully. Some strategies work on short-term trades as well as long-term trades. The type of Forex strategies you choose depends on a few factors like:

•**Entry points - traders need to determine the appropriate time to enter the market**

•**Exit point-trader need to develop rules on when to exit the market as well as how to get out of a losing position**

•**Time availability**

If you have a full-time job, then you cannot use day trading or scalping styles

•**Personal choices**

People who prefer lower winning rates but larger gains should go for position trading while those who prefer higher winning rate but smaller gains can choose the swing trading

Common Forex Trading strategies include:

1.Range trading strategy   Range trading is one of the many viable trading strategies. This strategy is where a trader identifies the support and resistance levels and buys at the support level and sells at the resistance level.

This strategy works when there is a lack of market direction or the absence of a trend. Range trading strategies can be broken down into three steps:

•Finding the Range

Finding the range uses the support and resistance zones. The support zone is the buying price of the security while the resistance zone price is the selling price of a security. A breakout happens in the event that the price goes beyond the trading range, whereas a breakdown occurs in the event that the price goes below the trading range.

•Time Your Entry

Traders use a variety of indicators like price action and volume to enter and exit the trading range. They can also use oscillators like CCI, RSI, and stochastics to time their entry. The oscillators track prices using mathematical calculations. Then the traders wait for the prices to reach the support or resistance zones. They often strike when the momentum turns price in the opposing direction.

•Managing Risk

The last step is risk management. When the level of support or resistance breaks, traders will want to exit any range-based positions. They can either use a stop loss above the previous high or invert the process with a stop below the current low.

Pros

•There are ranges that can last even for years producing multiple winning trades.

Cons

•Long-lasting ranges are not easy to come by, and when they do, every range trader wants to use it.

•Not all ranges are worth trading

2.Trend Trading Strategy

Another popular and common Forex Trading strategy is the trend trading strategy. This strategy attempts to make profits by analyzing trends. The process involves identifying an upward or downward trend in a currency price movement and choosing trade entry and exit points based on the currency price within the trend.

Trend traders use these four common indicators to evaluate trends; moving averages, relative strength index (RSI), On-Balance-Volume (OBV), and Moving Average Convergence Divergence (MACD). These indicators provide trend trade signals, warn of reversals, and simplify price information. A trader can combine several indicators to trade.

Pros

•Offers a better risk to reward

•Can be used across any markets

Cons

•Learning to trade on indicators can be challenging.

3.Pairs Trade

This is a neutral trading strategy, which allows pair traders to gain profits in any market conditions. This strategy uses two key strategies:

•Convergence trading - this strategy focuses on two historically correlated securities, where the trader buys one asset forward and sells a similar asset forward for a higher price anticipating that prices will become equal. Profits are made when the underperforming position gains value, and the outperforming position's price deflates

•Statistical trading - this is a short-term strategy that uses the mean reversion models involving broadly diversified Security Portfolios. This strategy uses data mining and statistical methods.

Pros

•If pair trades go as expected investors can make profits

Cons

•This strategy relies on a high statistical correlation between two securities, which can be a challenge.

•Pairs trade relies a lot on historical trends, which do not depict future trends accurately.

4.Price Action Trading

This Forex Trading strategy involves analyzing the historical prices of securities to come up with a trading strategy. Price action trading can be used in short, medium, and long periods. The most commonly used price action indicator is the price bar, which shows detailed information like high and low-price levels during a specific period. However, most traders use more than one strategy to recognize trading patterns, stop-losses, and entry, and exit levels. Technical analysis tools also help price action traders make decisions.

Pros

•**No two traders will interpret certain price action the same way**

Cons

•**Past price history cannot predict future prices accurately**

5.Carry Trade Strategy

Carry trade strategy involves borrowing a low-interest currency to buy a currency that has a high rate; the goal is to make a profit with the interest rate difference. For example, one can buy currency pairs like the Japanese yen (low interest) and the Australian dollar (high interest) because the interest rate spreads are very high. Initially, carry trade was used as a one-way trade that moved upwards without reversals, but carry traders soon discovered that everything went downhill once the trade collapsed.

With the carry trade strategy:

1.You need to first identify which currencies offer high rates and which ones have low rates.

2.Then match two currencies with a high-interest differential

3.Check whether the pair has been in an upward tendency favoring the higher-interest rate currency

Pros

•The strategy works in a low volatility environment.

•Suitable for a long-term strategy

•Cons

•Currency rates can change anytime

•Ricky because they are highly leveraged

•Used by many traders therefore overcrowded

6.Momentum Trading

This strategy involves buying and selling assets according to the strength of recent price trends. The basis for this strategy is that an asset price that is moving strongly in a given direction will continue to move in the same direction until the trend loses strength. When assets reach a higher price, they tend to attract many investors and traders who push the market price even higher. This continues until large pools of sellers enter the market and force the asset price down Momentum traders identify how strong trends are in a given direction.

They open positions to take advantage of the expected price change and close positions when the prices go down.

There are two kinds of momentum:

•Relative momentum - different securities within the same class are compared against each other, and then traders and investors buy strong performing ones and sell the weak ones.

•Absolute momentum - an asset's price is compared against its previous performance.

Pros

•Traders can capitalize on volatile market trends

•Traders can gain high profit over a short period

•This strategy can take advantage of changes in stock prices caused by emotional investors.

Cons

•A momentum investor is always at a risk of timing a buy incorrectly.

•This strategy works best in a bull market; therefore, it is market sensitive

•This strategy is time-intensive; investors need to keep monitoring the market daily.

•Prices can shift in a different direction anytime

7.Pivot Points

This strategy determines resistance and support levels using the average of the previous trading sessions, which predict the next prices. They take the average of the high, low, and closing prices. A pivot point is a price level used to indicate market movements. Bullish sentiment occurs when one trades above the pivot point while bearish sentiment occurs when one trades below the pivot point.

Pros

•Traders can use the levels to plan out their trading in advance because prices remain the same throughout the day

•Works well with other strategies

Cons

•Some traders do not find pivot points useful

•There is no guarantee that price will stop or reverse at the levels created on the chart

8.Fundamental Analysis

This strategy involves analyzing the economic, social, and political forces that may affect the supply and demand of an asset. Usually, people use supply and demand to gauge which direction the price is headed to. The Fundamental analysis strategy then analyzes any factors that may affect supply and demand. By assessing these factors, traders can determine markets with a good economy and those with a bad one.

Forex Strategies for Beginners

When starting on Forex Trading, it important to keep things simple. As a beginner, avoid thinking about money too much and focus on one or two strategies at a time. The following three strategies are easy to understand and perfect for beginners.

1.Inside Bar Trading Strategy

This highly effective strategy is a two-bar price action strategy with an inside bar and a prior/mother bar. The inside bar is usually smaller and within the high and low range of the prior bar. There are many variations of the inside bar, but what remains constant is that the prior bar always fully engulfs the inside bar. Although very profitable, the inside bar setup does not occur often.

There are two main ways you can trade using inside bars:

•As a continuation move - This is the easiest way to trade inside bars. The inside bars are traded in trending markets following the direction of the trend.

•As a reversal pattern - the inside bars are traded counter-trend

When using this strategy, it is important to look for these characteristics when evaluating the pattern:

•Time frame matters - avoid any time frame less than the daily.

•Focus on the breakout - best inside bar trades happen after a break of consolidation where the preceding trend is set to resume.

•The trend Is your friend - trading with the trend is the only way to trade an inside bar

•A favorable risk to reward ratio is needed when trading an inside bar

•The size of the inside bar in comparison to the prior bar is extremely important

2.Pin Bar Trading Strategy

This strategy is highly recommended for beginners because it is easy to learn due to a better visual representation of price action on a chart. It is one of the easiest strategies to trade. Pin bars show a reversal in the market and, therefore, can be useful in predicting the direction of the price.

There are various ways traders trading with pin bars can enter the market:

•At the current market price

•Using an on-stop entry

•At limit entry, which is at the 50% retrace of the pin bar

To improve your odds when using the pin bar strategy:

•Trade with the trend

•Wait for a break of structure

•Trade from an area of value

Some of the mistakes pin bar traders should avoid include the following:

•Assuming the market will reverse because of a pin bar

•Focus too much on the pin bars and miss out on other trading opportunities

•All pin bars are not the same and should not be treated as such

3.Forex Breakout Strategy

A breakout strategy is where investors find stocks that have built strong support or resistance level, wait for a breakout, and enter the market when momentum is in their favor. This strategy is important because it can offer expansions in volatility, major price moves, and limited risk. A breakout occurs when the price moves beyond the support or resistance level. The breakout strategy is good for beginners because they can catch every trend in the market. Breakouts occur in all types of market environments.

Traders establish a bullish position when prices are set to close above a resistance level and a bearish position when prices close below a support level. Sometimes traders can be caught on a false breakout, and the only way to determine if it is a false breakout is to wait for confirmation. False breakout prices usually go beyond the support and resistance level; however, they return to a prior trading range by the end of the day.

Good investors plan how they will exit the markets before establishing a position. With breakouts, there are two exit plans:

•Where to exit with profit-traders can assess the stock recent behaviors to determine reasonable objectives. When traders meet their goals, they can exit the position. They can either raise a stop-loss to lock in profits or exit a portion of the position to let the rest run

•Where to exit with a loss - breakout trading show traders clearly when a trade has failed, and therefore they can determine where to set stop-loss order. Traders can use the old support or resistance level to close a losing trade

Pros

•You can catch every trend in the market

••Prices can quickly move in your favor

Cons

•Traders can get caught in a false breakout

•It can be difficult to enter a trade

Tips for trading breakouts:

•Never sell on breakdown or buy on breakout both carry extreme risks

•Trade with the trend

•Wait for higher volume to confirm a breakout

•Take advantage of volatility cycles

•Enter on the retest of support or resistance

•Have a predetermined exit plan

Note

Beginners are more likely to be successful in trade than their experienced counterparts are because they have not yet cultivated any bad habits. Experienced traders have to break bad habits and put aside any emotions built over the years.

Price Analysis

In this chapter, we are going to be talking about technical analysis and fundamental analysis. It is essential that you understand these two concepts, as they will help you tremendously with the growth of your Forex trading endeavors. Both of these techniques work very well when it comes to helping you make more profits out of your trading endeavors. Nonetheless, they both have their places. That being said, we will talk about technical analysis and explain to you what it is and the same thing with the fundamental analysis. And then we will help you understand which method works better for what, once you've been able to understand this you will be in a much better position in terms of making more money with Forex Trading.

Technical analysis

To put with technical analysis is, it is a way Forex Traders find a framework to study the price movement. The simple theory behind this method is that a person will look at the previous prices and the changes, hence determine the current trading conditions and the potential price movement. The only problem with this method would be that it is theoretical meaning that all technical analysis is that it is reflected in the price. The price reflects the information which is out there, and the price action is all you would need to make a trade. The technical analysis banks on history and the trends, and the Traders will keep an eye on the past, and they will keep an eye on the future as well and based on that they will decide if they want to trade or not.

More importantly, the people who are going to be trading using the technical analysis will use history to determine whether they're going to make the trade or not. Essentially the way to check out technical analysis would be to look up the trading price of a particular currency in five years. This is what many Forex Traders used to determine the history and the future of the currency, and whether or not they should trade using technical analysis. There are many charts you can look up online to figure out how technical analysis takes place. However, we have given you a brief explanation of what technical analysis is. When using technical analysis, they also look at the trends that took place in the past. Most of the time, the currency fluctuates simply because of the trends that took place at that time, keeping that in mind, the Traders will look at the future and see if the trends will retake the place. If so, then they will most definitely trade or not trade depending on that's going to benefit them or not. Even though many people would consider technical analysis very "textbook," it is still very subjective. The reason why it is very personal is it because people interpret things differently. Some might think that the past will help the currency, whereas some might think it won't. Which is why technical analysis is both textbook and subjective at the same time. The reason why it is textbook is that you have to do a lot of research before you pull the trigger, and it is subjective because the final decision it's going to be based on how you feel about the trade. Many people say that technical analysis as more of a short-term thing; however, some still believe the technical report can be used in the long-term.

In our opinion, we think that technical analysis short. The reason why we think technical analysis is short-term is that we are mainly basing our assumptions based on the past and the trends that took place.

Keeping that in mind, the capital gains you might see from technical analysis might be short-term. Meaning that the tray that you will make will not keep going in the long-term and will be a quick gain for you. Keeping that in mind, technical analysis is a great tool to use for people who are looking to make more money from Forex Trading rather quickly, however, make sure that you do research properly on the currency before you make a trade on it. Many people make a trade on it by looking at the 5-year chart. However, it's much deeper than that you need to make sure that the trends that took place during those five years are going to retake the place. If not, then it will be entirely subjective for you to make a trade or not. The great thing about technical analysis would be that if you do it correctly, you will have a better chance of seeing success from it, and it can build a ton of confidence in new traders. This will be a significant thing for newbies or could be a bad thing for them since you will become extremely confident and make a blunder.

Fundamental analysis

Fundamental analysis is more realistic and feasible in the long term. The whole premise behind the fundamental analysis is that you look at the economy of the country and the trading system that's going on to determine whether it is a good trade or not. More focusing on economics, that's why it helps you to figure out which dollar is going up or down and what is causing it. One of the greatest things you can do when it comes to Forex Trading is to understand why a dollar is dropping or going up. Once you're able to understand that, you will be in a much better position for gaining profits in your Forex Trading endeavors. When using the fundamental analysis, you will be looking at the country's employment and unemployment rate also see how the training with different countries overall sing the country's economy before you decide on whether you should try it or not. Many successful Forex Traders solely believe in fundamental analysis, as it is factual, unlike technical analysis. Even though technical analysis is accurate, it is not guaranteed like the theoretical analysis. Instead of looking at the trends, you will be looking at what is causing the highs and the lows. Not only that, based on the highs and lows, you will be able to determine the country's current and future economic outlook, whether it is good or not. One rule of thumb to look into with be how good the country is doing, the better the country is doing, the more foreign investors are going to take part in it. Once starting the piece in it, the dollar or the currency in that country will go up tremendously. The idea behind fundamental analysis is that you need to look at the country's economical and you also need to look at. To make you understand, what fundamental analysis is it is mostly when you invest in a country is doing well in the economy, and not invest in a company when they're doing bad in the marketplace. Which makes sense since the economy dictates how high are low prices going to be per dollar. Most of the time, investors will invest the money as soon as they see the dollar going up. The reason why they will do that is that they know the dollar will keep climbing up since the economy is getting better.

One of the great examples would be when the US dollar dropped in 2007 2008, and the Canadian dollar took up, at that point, a lot of investors are investing in Canadian dollars of the US dollar. After a very long time, the US dollar

was dropping tremendously, whereas the Canadian dollar was more expensive than the US dollar. This was one of the anomalies which took place back in the day. If you were to use technical analysis in this instance, then you will not get a lot of success out of this economy drop. Which is why fundamental analysis could work a lot better or most people in the long-term and in the short-term, which is why many top traders recommend you follow fundamental analysis instead of technical analysis to find out which dollar you're going to be investing in.

Which method to use and when?

Now we get into the part where we show you which method to use and when ideally when you're Forex Trading you would like to dabble with technical analysis and fundamental analysis to see optimal success. However, you can do fundamental analysis and see progress, both long-term and short-term. In our opinion the best way to go about it would be to try out technical analysis in the short-term, the reason why we think the technical analysis in short would work very good for you is that it is something that you can't go wrong with if you do it properly. As we explained to you what technical analysis is, you can see why it is so good for someone to start with technical analysis and to see amazing results out of it.

Another thing technical analysis can help you out with would be that it will help you to build up your confidence in the beginning. When you're starting Forex Trading especially in the beginning, it is essential that you build up confidence and you make yourself believe that you can, make money from Forex Trading. This will help you to continue with your Forex Trading journey and to learn more, more accurately help you to start investing your money the right way and to continue off becoming a full-time Forex Trader. Once you have dabbled with technical analysis, you can start doing your more long-term trades with fundamental analysis. The only problem with fundamental analysis would be that there's a lot more research to be done, and if you're trying to make Forex Trading a long-term income Source or a full-time income Source, then the chances are you should be doing your research before you make a trade. Keep in mind that, fundamental analysis will help you to keep going in the long-term and will yield you the best results possible. Even though technical analysis has a higher success rate, fundamental analysis will be a lot more long-term. Secondly, the more you do fundamental analysis, the easier it's going to get for you. Keeping that in mind, the best method to go about Forex Trading, in the beginning, would be to start with technical analysis make small trades, and make some money. This will help you to build up your confidence with Forex Trading and therefore help you to keep going on. The second thing you should be doing is research on the fundamental analysis I'm slowly started dabbing with it until you are sure on which dollar or currency on investing based on your research. You will require some brain power to really dabble with Forex Trading using fundamental analysis. However, once you understand it and start dabbling with it, you will see the success they looking for with Forex Trading. The final verdict would be to use both of them however used technical analysis, in the beginning, to really see some short-term benefits out of it and then eventually branch off to fundamental analysis and then dabbing our technical analysis trading there to see the small incremental games. When combined both you will be in a much better position to make a lot of money from Forex Trading.

Risk And Managment

The truth is, along with the basics, this is perhaps the one thing that will ensure your success more than anything else. Consider this: **Great risk management can mitigate a mediocre strategy but poor risk management will certainly ruin a great strategy.**

If you're familiar with trading and have read multiple books on the subject, chances are most of them boil risk management down to your risk per trade, stop loss and position size etc. The reward risk ratio is often presented as the catch all solution to understanding risk management. The truth is the risk reward ratio of your strategy is merely the starting point. Risk in trading contains both quantitative and qualitative aspects. In this chapter, my aim is to enlighten you on both aspects of this. First, let us look at the quantitative aspect.

Quantitative Risk

Any trading strategy, if it needs to be successful, needs to have an edge. This edge can be measured at it most basic level using 2 key statistics, namely, the reward/risk ratio (hereby referred to as R) and your win rate percentage. Most traders get hung up on either one of these numbers and neglect to understand that these 2 work in tandem. One affects the other. A typical newbie is someone who aspires to a 100% win rate and a 5R+ ratio. This is some Alice in Wonderland level of thinking and is practically impossible.

The more realistic way of approaching this is to first of all determine, given your R per trade, what is the minimum win rate you need to break even? Notice I said break even, not make millions. Your first goal, if you're struggling for consistency and to make money, is to simply break even. **The progression usually goes as follows: losing lots of money--> losing a little--> break even--> making a little money-->making lots of money**. You cannot aspire to jump to the highest level directly if you're stuck in the lowest level. There is no jumping steps with trading. You need to put in the work and only focus on what you need to do next. The calculation for this break even rate is fairly simple. If you're making 2R per win (that is, you're making on average, twice the amount you lose on average, every time you have a winning trade), you will need a win percentage of around 35%. The calculation is pretty simple: say on 10 trades you win 3 and lose 7 with 2R per win. So your losses come to (7*1)= 7R. Your winners come to (3*2)= 6R. Your profit and loss is 6R-7R= -1R. So if you're risking 2% per trade, over 10 trades you can expect to lose 2% with this strategy. Now, its important to note, when starting out, you will not have much of a base to calculate these numbers. You will need a minimum of 100 trades to reasonably calculate these ratios with accuracy. Therefore, my advice when you've placed under 100 trades is to risk as little as possible on your trades. I personally risk 0.5% per trade. There are a lot of trading authorities out there which say risking 2% per trade is perfectly fine but this is hogwash. You will find the vast majority of professional and successful traders risk anywhere from 0.25% to 1% per trade. The successful trader who risks 2% is an outlier.

Your first action upon reading that would probably have been to do some quick mental math and realize you cannot make millions a year with your capital size by doing that. This is indicative of a flawed mindset which needs some fixing. The good news is it doesn't take much to fix this. The truth is, the correct approach to trading is to constantly cover your downside all the time. Most people only think of the upside and their winners. The successful trader always covers risk and the downside before turning her attention to the upside.

Those of you familiar with the writings of Benjamin Graham may recognize this thought process. This is nothing but the "Margin of Safety" in action. This is a principle which is good enough for some of the greatest investors of all time. It ought to be good enough for you as well. There's no need to waste time reinventing the wheel. Just follow the process and you will get there. Those of you worrying about how you will get rich with this sort of trading, please be patient.

Getting back to our quantitative look at risk, once you've placed at least 100 trades risking under 0.25% per trade, you will be able to have relevant stats on your strategy and trade process. As I said previously, the win rate and R is the bare minimum you have to look at. You need to further dig into your numbers and understand the variance of your results. I'm not going to bore you with the statistical definition of variance but will instead illustrate what this practically means.

Let's say you're on a losing streak. Indeed if your trading strategy has a win rate of 35%, you will lose far more than you win and losing streaks of 2-3 trades are extremely likely. This is where struggling traders fail. Once the losing streak starts, they start tinkering with the strategy, assuming something is wrong. This is indicative of a Holy Grail mindset and as I've mentioned previously, this is completely the wrong way to go about trading. **The correct approach is to understand what are the odds of such a losing steak occurring?**

That is, with a 35% win rate, what are the odds of having a losing streak of 2 trades? 3 trades? 10 trades? I'm not going to disclose the answers to those questions here because once you search for them yourself, you're likely to be shocked. Briefly, it is extremely likely you will have a losing streak of at least 8 trades with a win rate of 35%. Only when your losing streak becomes of such a size that it is improbable, should you start looking at your trade process. Until then, you need to remain aware of what your odds are at all times.

This is what it means to think in probabilities in trading. Most authorities simply make that statement and leave it hanging without further explanation. Trading is about being aware of your probabilities at all times. I even gave examples of when a given strategy fails. This is because I'm not concerned with how much of a sure shot a strategy is. I'm only concerned with what the win rate needs to be and how much R do I need to make on that strategy to make money. If I cannot make those numbers work for me after a sizeable sample, I drop it. This is how a professional thinks and it is crucial for you to adopt this method of thinking.

Understanding variance is a key part of evaluating your current strategy. Its not all doom and gloom though. For all the odds of a losing streak there are odds of a win streak as well. The number of wins in the streak will be smaller of course but when you factor in the 2R reward per win, you're making pretty good money on those streaks. I'll bet none of you will mind experiencing variance via a win streak. You shouldn't mind experiencing it via a losing streak either. Another key variable to look for is the consistency of your risk management. Now this can't be boiled down to a number but basically, you need to look at your losses and check if they are consistently around your risk percent per trade. So if you've decided to risk 0.25% of your account per trade, how many losing trades are actually at or below this number? If your losers are all over the place but average out to 0.25%, that is frankly, terrible risk management. It means you're likely adding to your losers and engaging in wishful and emotional thinking every time you enter a trade. The successful trader is someone whose losses show a consistent risk percentage of their account. So if they decide to risk 0.25%, their losses will be 0.25% or less. Enforcing discipline in this regard will do wonders for your strategy. Another bogus piece of advice I've seen floating around recently is the thought that you should risk a fixed amount per trade versus a fixed percentage of your account. Risking a fixed amount violates the very basis of risk management which is covering your downside. It means in a losing streak you're actually risking a bigger percentage of your account and in a win streak you will be risking a smaller percentage as the streak lengthens. This is getting the worst of both worlds: losing more in a losing streak and winning less in a win streak. I really hope I don't need to further explain how stupid this piece of advice is. Some proponents of this method will argue it gets you out of draw downs (that is, when your account balance dips below its peak equity value) faster. My response is, draw down recovery is a function of variance, not some BS risk per trade formula. Since we're on the subject, draw downs are an important statistic to measure as well. No account in the world is on a continuous upward 45 degree angle. You will have peaks and valleys. A draw down is essentially the length of that dip, measured as a percentage from the peak equity value and also as time, that is, measuring it in days and months. You will also need to measure recovery time which is the length of the upward swing past the old equity high from the bottom measured in days. A good system will have a faster recovery time as compared to the draw down time.   The percentage of draw down matters as well. As an FX trader, you should be aiming for less than 5% draw down per month. If you're starting out, I recommend a draw down limit of 3%. Yes, that is a limit. It means you will stop trading when you breach it. You need to have a draw down limit for a day, week and month. Your daily limit can be defined as either a percentage or as the number of consecutive losses. For example if you lose 6 in a row, you cease trading for the day. I'm not saying 6 is a magic number, you will need to work out how much that means as a loss percentage given your risk per trade. Enforcing this requires discipline and awareness. Violate this and you will not succeed. Its really as simple as that. If you're still not convinced consider this: Even Usain Bolt had bad days at the track. What makes you think you will have only good days in the market? Recognize when things are bad and exercise the option Bolt never had. You have the choice to take part or sit out.

Another informative statistic is the length of winners and losers measured as the time the trade was active. If your losers are far shorter in time than your winners, for example, perhaps you're placing your stops too close and not giving your trades room to breathe. Also look at how long your losers were in positive territory. If the majority of your losers, for example, tend to reach around 1.5R and then turn back, either your stops are too wide or perhaps you'd be better off targeting 1.5R instead of a higher ratio. You will be compensated because you'll have a higher win rate.

Qualitative Risk

Looking at risk qualitatively is a bit more difficult for beginners since most of them have never thought of risk in such terms or ever thought of risk as a function of discipline. Indeed most unsuccessful traders, whether beginners or experienced, tend to think of trading as having a successful strategy. They do not pay heed to risk management or mindset. They define an "edge" as how often the strategy wins or how much better it is or how it is some secret sauce that no one has discovered. The reality is, in this age of constant information, it is impossible for some secret sauce to exist indefinitely. Successful trading is indeed having an edge. Your edge, though, is made up of a number of things. It means executing your strategy perfectly. It means risking the correct amounts per trade. Successfully executing this edge is a matter of preparation. Ask yourself, how well do you prepare for your trading day? Do you roll out of bed an hour before the open and sit down munching your breakfast and coffee while looking at your charts?

Do you even consider things such as: How well did you sleep? How physically fit are you? What is your current mental state? Are you going through a tough period in your life that needs addressing? Have you practiced your technical skills? Are you aware of how your weaknesses will attack you today? And so on.

Make no mistake, to trade successfully you need to approach your trading day with as much precision as an athlete approaches game day. Using the previous example of Usain Bolt, do you really think he ever showed up to a race hungover? Do you really think he didn't practice extensively before hand and execute his workout strategy? Do you think he ignored his nutrition needs? (notwithstanding his claim of eating Mcdonalds). Do you think he was out until 3 A.M the day before a race? Most of all, do you think he changed his methods of preparation simply because he was having a bad day? Do you think he did things differently before every race or did he do the exact same things over and over again?

These questions answer themselves. If you think you do not need to prepare for your trading day, you might as well flush your money down the toilet, you'll at least learn a lesson that way. Preparing well gives us confidence in our abilities and lessens the impact of losses since we know deep down there isn't anything we could have done better. It gives us a marker as to where our abilities are and what we need to do next. So what constitutes as good preparation?

To sum it up in a sentence: You need to ensure your mind is as close to its peak cognitive ability as possible. There will always be distractions and tough periods in our lives but you have to make sure you have a way to put them aside when trading. You need to evaluate if you have the ability to do this. The death of a loved one, for example, is impossible to put aside for most people. An argument with your spouse/girl/boyfriend though is somewhat more manageable for most. The point is you need to be aware of yourself and make a call. I highly recommend engaging in physical exercise and some form of meditation or mindfulness prior to the trading session. This ensures our bodies and minds get a workout and it refreshes us. I don't believe I need to go into detail about the benefits of exercise and meditation. Ensure you get quality sleep every night. Do what you need to do to ensure this. If you miss exercising for a day, you can get by. Miss a night's sleep though and you're effectively a zombie. Take some time during the day to also practice your strategy. There will be core elements to it and keep reinforcing and practicing these basics. Should you choose to follow the trend strength approach, you will need to constantly practice this skill in the beginning. The best way to practice is on a simulation software or on a demo account, although the latter is a bit slower in terms of reps received. As you can see, not executing these steps correctly will leave you below your peak ability and trading without taking care of these things is akin to jumping into a sea of sharks with bloody meat strapped to you. Execute these to the best of your abilities and don't worry about anything else. If your mind is too unfocused simply walk away and come back the next day. The market won't go anywhere. If you choose to ignore this aspect, you're running huge risks and no amount of quantitative statistics will save you.

Your Trading Plan

One of the most important things of the trader needs to do is they need to develop a trading plan. Typically, most traders don't develop a trading plan. Instead what they do, is they trade on-the-fly. Now let's consider is what we talked about in the last section. I am sure that most readers are going to agree that the type of person that would scoff at using a demo platform for couple weeks to learn the basics of trading, is also going to be the same person that fails to develop a trading plan. Well, let's consider the following. Concerning determining your success or failure as a Forex trader, having a trading plan is going to be one of the most important factors. Simply put, having a trading plan is one of the most important things that you are going to need to get you a handle on when becoming a new Forex trader. So what are some of the things that are going to go into Forex trading plan? The first item that you should, including your plan, is the balance you intend to keep in your Forex trading account. Keep in mind that when I say balance, I mean the total of cash plus positions held. So no matter what it is, let's say, $5000 or $10,000, pick a number to stick with for the next three months at least. Of course, if you find out that you are a successful Forex trader, you are going to want to increase the amount in your balance. So having a balance enforces a bit of discipline with your account. First of all, if you end up taking some losses, you should stick to your plan and as soon as it's available deposit more money in the balance to bring it up to the level that you have determined.

So if you set out and determine that you want to balance of $5000, and you take a loss, and your balance drops to $4000, stick to your plan and add another $1000 to the balance. However, in your first year of trading, I don't believe that you should add money to your account on a whim. You can reevaluate the situation every three months and adjust, as necessary. But for the three-month period, maintain the balance at the level that you have determined. The key point here is to avoid letting emotion drive you into pouring money into Forex trading out of excitement. Sometimes new traders get overwhelmed by excitement; maybe they've made a trade that is earning money. Amid their excitement, they might drain their bank account to fund more trades. And what happens more often than not is they end up getting into losing trades, because they are overexcited, and then they find themselves in a position where they have lost money. So besides the amount of money that you're going to invest, let's take a look at some of the other things that we need to consider including a trading plan. The first thing that I would mention is you should have a goal for profits. At first, we aren't necessarily talking about actually meeting the goal. But you need to have a good idea of where you are going so that you can take steps to correct your course, if you are not moving in the right direction. Second, your initial goals of profit should be modest. I know that many traders are anxious to get going, and they would love to drop their day job. But to have a realistic chance of doing that, unless you happen to be a whiz at trading, it's probably best to start off with small goals that you actually have a chance of meeting, and then each time you meet the goal, you can elevate to a new level.

So maybe you start small, like shooting for a profit of $500 over the course of a month. Once you meet the goal, you could raise the level. So using this example maybe after you have reached $500, then you change it to $1000. Over time, you'll find that soon enough you will be able to get in the situation where you are actually able to trade for a full-time living. The next thing that we need to put in our trading plan, our fixed loss, and profit levels. This is going to be highly important for the purposes of enforcing discipline. It's only going to be up to you, so I can tell you what to do in order to be successful, but I can't be there with you when you make your trades. So some readers are going to read this and nod, but not follow the advice. If that's you, more than likely, you are not going to end up as a successful trader. So you should take a level of profit that you are willing to accept and be happy about. This can be done in absolute terms, or it could be done in percentage terms. If we are talking about absolute terms, then you could set up a level of pips that you're willing to accept as a profitable move. Or as a percentage, you simply set the percentage gain or return on investment you're willing to accept with each trade. This is not something you are going to write down and then file away. Rather, you need to make this a rule that you follow with every single trade that you enter. Many platforms allow you to set up take profit levels with the trade. So you can use that feature and put a take profit order which is a limit order and then have it automatically executed. By the same token, you should figure out a maximum loss that you are willing to except on each trade. This can be done on a percentage basis. Then with every trade that you enter, you can enter a stop-loss order, so that it is automatically executed.

The next thing that should be included in your trading plan is a list of currency pairs you're going to focus on. In addition, your trading plan should include the main strategy that you're going to use for most of your trades.

Keep in mind that your trading plan does not have to be written in stone. But I would advise sticking to it for at least three months. So each quarter, you can revise the trading plan as you see fit. But then stick to it for three months, so that you can give it enough time to find out if it's working or not.

Choosing Your Broker

A broker refers to a firm or somewhat an individual who charges a certain fee or rather a commission for executing the buying and the selling process. In other words, they play the role of connecting the customer and the seller of the product. Thus, they are generally paid for acting as a link between the two parties. For instance, a client might be willing to buy shares from a particular organization. However, he might be lacking enough information about the places that he can purchase these shares. Thus, he will be forced to seek a person who understands well the stock exchange markets. The broker will, therefore, educate the client as well as link them with the right sellers. The broker will thus earn by offering such a connection. Other brokers sell insurance policies to individuals. In most cases, the individuals earn a commission once the clients they brought in the organization buy or renews the system. Any insurance companies have utilized the aspect as a way of increasing their sales.

List Of Common Brokers

IG

It is rated as one of the best Forex brokers in the world. It was one of the pioneers in offering contracts for difference as well as spread beating. The organization was founded in the year 1974 and had been growing as a leader in online trading as well as the marketing industry. One of the aspects that have boosted its growth is the fact that it has linked a lot of customers, hence gaining more trust.

In other words, a duet to its large customer base, a lot of clients prefers selling and buying their services. The other aspect worth noting is that this organization is London based, and it is among one of the companies that are listed on the London Stock Exchange market for more than 250 times. The aspect is due to the fact that it offers more than 15,000 products across several asset classes. Such classes include CFDs on shares, Forex, commodities, bonds, crypto currencies as well as indices. Another aspect worth noting is that the 2019 May report, the firm is serving more than 120,000 active clients around the globe. Also, there are more than 350,000 clients that are served on a daily basis. The aspect has been critical in boosting its expansion as this group of individuals does more advertisements. Some of the benefits that one gains by working in this industry are the fact that it allows comprehensive trading and the utilization of tools that enhance the real exchange of data. The other aspect worth noting is that it has a public traded license that allows a regular jurisdiction across the entire globe. In other words, one can acquire the services of this organization across the whole world with ease without the fear of acting against the laws of the nation. Also, the premises offer some of the competitive based commission that enhances pricing as spreading of Forex. There is also a broad range of markets that are associated with the premises too, there several currencies and multi assets CFDs that are offered by the organization. The aspect has been critical in the sense that it allows the perfect utilization of all the services as well as the resources available across the globe. Some of the services that are offered by the organization are permitted globally, such that even after traveling from one nation to the other, one can still access their services. Since the year 1974, the organization has joined more than 195,000 traders across the entire globe. The aspect has allowed the selling its shares as well as services hence its fame.

Saxo Bank

The Forex broker was established in 1992and has then been among the leading organization in offering Forex services as well as the multi-asset brokerages across more than 15 nations. Some of these nations include the UK, Denmark, and Singapore, among others. One of the aspects of the organization is that it offers services to both retailers as well as institutional clients in the globe. The character has allowed the premises to provide more than one million transactions each day. Thus, it holds over $ 16 billion in asset management. The Saxo bank also offers more services to all of her clients. Such services include Spot FX, Non-deliverable Forwards (NDFs), contract difference as well as all the stock exchange options. The aspect has been critical in increasing its customer base across the globe. Some of the services such as crypto and bond services that are offered in the premises has allowed its expansion in the sense that they are sensitive and essentials. Some of the benefits that one gain by assessing the services of the premises are that it enhances diverse selection of quality, it increases competitive commissions and Forex spread as well as an improved multiple financial jurisdiction function that is allowed across the entire globe. In other words, the premises offer services that are allowed in the whole world, and that considers the rules and policies provided in each nation. The aspect has enhanced its continued growth despite the increased competition.

One is required to pay a minimum deposit of about $2000 and an automated trading solution for all the traders. There are times when the premises offer bonuses of 182 trade Forex pairs to all its clients. The aspect has also been the key reason behind its increased expansion. In other words, there are various services offered at a relatively low price hence the widening of its customer base.

CMC Markets

The premises were founded in 1989 and since then, it has grown to be one of the leading retail forex as well as a CFD brokerage. The premises thus serve more than 10,000 CFD instruments that cut across all the classes such as Forex, commodities as well as security markets. The aspect has allowed the premises to spread its services to more than 60,000 clients across the entire globe. The premises have more than 15 offices that are well distributed in the nation; it offers the services. Most of its actions are thus related in UK, Australia as well as Canada. The aspect is due to the fact that the premises have it is customer bases in some of these nations. In other words, its serves are well are accepted in Canada and the UK. There are various benefits that one gains by joining the premises. One, the premise offers some of the best competitive spread to all her customers. In other words, there are a variety of services that one can choose from. Also, the premises offer some of the largest selection of currency pairs in the entire industry. There are more than one hundred and eighty currencies that one can access by joining the premises.

The other aspect worth noting is that the premises offer some of the best regulated financial agents in the entire globe. In other words, there are policies as well as rules that govern the provision of services in the world. Also, it is easy to identify the premises as there are potent charts as well as patterns that are used as recognition tools.

City Index

The Forex broker was founded in 1983 in the UK. Since then, the premises have gained popularity and has turned out to be one of the leading brokers in London. It is worth noting that in 2015, the premises acquired GAIN Capital Holding Company that enhanced its increased customer base. Since 2015, the premises have been providing traders with services such as CFDs and spreading-betting derivatives. The premises have been further expanding the Forex services with the acquisition of markets as well as FX solutions before gaining the capital market. Nowadays, the City Index has been operating as an independent brand under GAIN Capital in Asia as well as the UK. The aspect has allowed a multi-asset solution hence offering traders access to over 12,000 products across the global markets.

Some of the benefits that one gains part of the capital holding, a large selection of CFDs as well as regulated in several jurisdictions. The organization has tight spreads as well as low margins and fast execution. In others, the premises have been time from time, offering average ranges to all the clients; hence its increased customer base.

XTB Review

The organization was founded in Poland in the year 2002. Since then the organization has been well known for its Forex and CFDs brokerage. Since then, the organization has maintained its offices in several nations; it offers its services. The premise has been working as a multi-asset broker that is regulated in several centers, hence increasing their competitive advantage. The premises have been trading as multiple financial centers offering a lot of services to all her traders. With a wide range of more than 2000 functions, the premises have been trading in almost all nations hence an increase in its customer base. The premises also offer excellent services that have been the reason behind its expansion. One of the aspects that have made the Forex broker be thriving in such a competitive environment.

Signs Of Illegitimate Brokers

Although numerous brokers have been working in the Forex industry, the aspect of legitimacy has been an issue affecting the progress of some these premises. One of the elements that are considered is the vulnerability of the clients. In most cases premises illegitimate brokers tend to rob of their customers. Most of them are self-reliant and optimistic. Most of them operate above their financial knowledge, hence making numerous mistakes. Most of these organization record big loses as they are relatively weak in term of management. The organization offers a lot of transactions that tend to be cumbersome in terms of management. It is worth noting that most of their operations aren't legitimate and never approved by the necessary authorities. Thus, when deciding on the kind of Forex premises to seek services from, it is essential to consider some factors.

Avoid assumptions that are exaggerative in terms of offering services that are above their knowledge. The aspect is harmful in the sense that they provide services that are not well planned hence recording a number of loses that befalls many clients in the long run. In other words, the drops recorded in the organization

Signs Of Legitimate Brokers

Although there are numerous illegitimate brokers in the market, there are legitimate brokers who offer excellent services. Most of them provide a few unique functions. In other words, they don't give a lot of transactions. Thus, they are able to manage their operations and command profits on their premises. The other aspect worth noting is that most of the services are approved by both the clients as well as the governing bodies in the organization. The other issue worth noting is that most of these premises have employed excellent knowledge in a range the progress of the customers. In other words, all their services are focused on advancing the clients.   In a nutshell, when selecting a Forex broker, it is good to consider several factors. It is critical to find whether the premises are approved by both the governments as well as the clients. It is good to view the number of services as well as the transactions that are offered by the premise. The aspect is due to the fact that most of the wrong assumptions tend to provide numerous services that are poorly managed. The reviews offered by the clients of each of these premises need to be considered as they reflect whether the brokers are legitimate or not. Clients of consistent clients tend to offer reviews that are good as the services they receive manage to be excellent.

The financial reports of these organization tend to be considered. The aspect is linked to the fact that they tend to reflect whether the brokers are making loses or profits. It is critical to find premises that record gains since the benefits tend to be high.

Choosing currency pairs

On stock exchanges, you trade stocks. On Forex, you trade currency, but the currency is always traded in pairs. It would be as if you had to own some stock, but if you were betting on Apple, you had to bet against Microsoft as well. On Forex, currencies are paired one against another such as the Euro against the U.S. Dollar, or the Australian Dollar against the Japanese Yen. Getting familiar with currency pairs and how they are displayed on the Forex markets is the first step in making your way around and understanding what you are doing.

Currency Pair Basics

A currency pair is listed with an abbreviation for the currency some of the most popular currencies include:

- USD: United States Dollar

- EUR: Euro

- JPY: Japanese Yen

- GBP: Great British Pound

- CHF: Swiss Franc

- CAD: Canadian Dollar

- AUD: Australian Dollar

- NZD: New Zealand Dollar

- MXN: Mexican Peso

- RUB: Russian Rubles

- CNY: China Yuan

- SGD: Singapore Dollar

Some currencies also go by nicknames. These include:

- USD: Greenback

- GBP: Cable or Sterling

- AUD: Aussie

- NZD: Kiwi

- CAD: Looney

- EUR: Chunnel

- CHF: Swiss

You should learn what the nicknames of the currencies are or have them referenced so that if you are in discussions about Forex or reading message boards, you have an idea of what people are talking about. If you are wondering where some of these strange names came from, some of them are historical. For example, in the early days of currency trading, undersea cables were used for electronic means of communication between Britain and the United States. That's where the name "cable" came from.

The Majors

Another important concept you need to know about is the majors. As you might guess, the majors are the currencies used by the major world economies. However, actually, the majors are expressed in pairs and they represent the most frequently traded currency pairs. The US Dollar is involved in something like 88% of all Forex trades and so more than $4 trillion per day of the currency trading on Forex involves the US Dollar.

The majors are:

- EUR/USD

- USD/JPY

- GBP/USD

- AUD/USD

- USD/CHF

- NZD/USD

- USD/CAD

These seven majors represent 85% of all currency trading. Notice that the United States Dollar is involved in every single one of the major currency pairs. The fact that these pairs represent most of the trading is important because that means that's where you are going to find the most liquidity. That could be significant if you are looking to exit a trade quickly. To complete a trade, you've got to find someone on the other end of it, willing to buy or sell as the case may be.

Many currencies from developing or third world countries are known as "exotics." While the majors are where most of the liquidity is, that doesn't mean you can't profit by trading exotics.

Currency pairs that aren't quoted against US Dollars are called cross-currency pairs. Each currency other than the US Dollar has its own set of cross currency pairs. All currencies trade against one another, but you can consider cross currency pairs just between the majors. For the Euro you have:

- EUR/GBP

- EUR/AUD

- EUR/NZD

- EUR/CAD

- EUR/CHF

- EUR/JPY

Since there are seven majors, all major currencies other than the US Dollar has six cross currency pairs with the other majors.

Currency Pairs Are Expressed in the Same Manner at All Times

You will notice that the currency pairs have one currency that comes first followed by the second currency. These are never changed so, if you are buying Euros and selling dollars, it's EUR/USD and if you are selling Euros and buying dollars, it's still EUR/USD. The first member of a pair is called the primary or the base currency and the second member of the pair is called the secondary, or the counter currency. This is just due to historical factors and for labeling purposes, it has nothing do with one currency's relation to the other in the modern world. In centuries past, the GBP was stronger than the US Dollar and so the currency pair has GBP listed first.

Note that on futures markets, the USD is always the secondary or counter currency. That doesn't just mean when the USD is in the currency pair, on the futures markets the USD is always the counter currency so while you'll see USD/JPY on the spot market, you'll see JPY/USD on the futures market. Again, when we are talking about Forex trading in this book, we are talking about the spot market. However, it's important to be aware of what you are looking at in case you happen to come across currency pairs from the futures markets.

Let's run through a few examples.

EUR/USD: The primary is the Euro, the secondary is the US Dollar.

USD/JPY: The primary is the US Dollar; the counter currency is the Japanese Yen.

MXN/JPY: The primary is the Mexican Peso, the secondary (or counter currency) is the Japanese Yen.

The Essence of Currency Pairs

Forex trading boils down to a competition between different currencies. You are trading one against the other and one is going to rise and one is going to fall. When you are using your trading platform, you're going to see listings of currency pairs displayed. EUR/USD is pitting the Euro against the US Dollar and you're betting for one and against the other. Of course, you're not guessing or using "hope," as a Forex trader you're studying the trends and sentiment in the market, using indicators and maybe paying some attention to macroeconomic news in order to make an educated forecast. That doesn't mean it's going to be right of course.

Let's see how this works. Remember that the pairs are always listed in the same order, so you'll have to understand what kind of trade you want to enter in order to pick one currency over the other.

Sticking with EUR/USD, let's say that you believe the Euro is going to rise against the dollar. That means that you're going to want to buy Euros and use your dollars to do it. After that, you hope that when you will sell your Euros, later on, you will get more dollars back than you had originally.

To bet on the Euro for EUR/USD – you are going to buy this currency pair. This means you believe the Euro is going to rise and the dollar is going to fall. Remember, everything in Forex is relative. Hence, that means we're saying that the Euro is going to rise compared to the USD. Let's look at some more examples to get some practice with this.

Consider USD/JPY. If you believe that the USD is going to rise and the Japanese Yen is going to fall relative to the dollar, then you will buy this currency pair.

If you believe the Mexican Peso is going to rise relative to the Japanese Yen, then you are going to buy the currency pair MXN/JPY.

Now, remember that the currency pairs are always listed in the same way. Otherwise, if you believe the USD is going to rise against the Euro, how is the transaction going to take place? In that case, you will sell the EUR/USD currency pair. Let's say this again:

Selling the EUR/USD currency pair means that you are betting that the USD is going to rise and the Euro is going to fall. When you sell this currency pair, you are selling Euros to buy dollars. Yes, it's confusing, because you probably think that you don't own any Euros. It doesn't matter; the broker/dealer is going to take care of everything for you automatically.

Trading Tools and Platform

A beginner's journey is already complex, so when the trader doesn't select the right platform, the difficulties increase. When the trading platform is easy to understand, you will not have difficulties when trying out new strategies and techniques on the demo account. There are many reliable brokers that you can select when you are trading Forex, but the problem is finding the ideal broker. To earn extra income, Forex is a good choice. But it doesn't mean Forex can be traded as the main source of income. However, either main income or part-time income, you must find the ideal broker and an excellent platform to keep going in trading. Even though there are many good brokers, you must do your research to find the right one that offers the most straightforward trading platform. I know, you will encounter difficulties when selecting the right broker, so let me help you. Before you settle for an ideal platform check whether the platform is reliable; it is one of the most crucial factors that you must consider when selecting a trading platform. You don't want to lose all the money that you collected, so make sure to find a platform that you can rely on. If you're going to deposit and withdraw your cash without facing any issues, the trading platform must be reliable.   Another important factor is charges related to the platform. You must consider the charges because your profits will disappear even before you know it if the charges are high. Besides, you are just starting your journey so your income will not be massive. The smaller income that you gain must be protected, so for that, you must consider the charges related to the trading platform.

You must next consider the licensing factor of the Forex platforms. If the relevant authorities monitor the platform, they are unlikely to fool you. The trading platforms will work according to terms and conditions, so you don't have to worry when you are trading through it. But to find whether the platform is licensed, you must do some research even if it is tough. Along with these, you must consider the simplicity in the Forex trading platform, but due to the software used, eventually, almost all the trading platforms have become easier to handle. In the meantime, don't forget to consider the leverage, margin, and other requirements that generally should be considered when selecting a trading platform. Once you select the ideal platform, you will be able to trade in a hassle-free way. However, there's more to learn about Forex trading platforms. So, keep reading!

There are two types of platforms, such as commercial and prop platforms. Before you pick any, you must ensure to understand the types in detail. Thus, prop platforms are designed by Forex brokers, and specialized companies develop commercial platforms. However, there are unique features for both the trading platforms. Even though the prop platforms are considerable, there are times when you might want to change the broker.

Beginners like you need a lot of time to get adjusted with the trading platform. But, I don't say trade execution speed is terrible because it is excellent in prop platforms, yet beginners will have a tough time understanding this platform.

So, beginners like you can consider the platforms designed by professional companies. One of the most common trading software is Metatrader. This is a user-friendly and high standard platform that you can consider even if you don't have experience. But if you are looking for a platform that includes broker feeds, then this is not going to help because the commercial platform has poor customization. These companies sell commercial platforms to Forex brokers so the benefits may be biased towards the broker, but not the trader. Yet, as beginners, you are not going to find anything better than commercial platforms because they are extremely user-friendly and flexible.

Now we will get into talking about the different platforms and techniques you can use in regards to starting your Forex Trading business. Keep in mind that there are many ways to begin trading using different platforms. We will recommend you some. However, it is your choice which platform you're going to be using for your Forex Trading. Overall, all of them work, and they will yield you the results that you're looking for when it comes to Forex Trading.

Nonetheless, there are over nine platforms what you can use for your Forex Trading needs. With that being said, we're going to go through all those nine trading platforms that will give you a better idea on which one to pick and our opinion on them. The first one we're going to talk about is going to be IG.

IG

This platform has known by many people to be one of the most trusted and well-planned out trading platforms to use for Forex Traders. Many of the top Forex Traders, use this platform for their Forex needs. They have a big list of tradable products and also provide you with excellent rating tools. They are known to be the top in the industry, with both trading tools and education. This is perhaps known to be the best trading platform for Forex traders to use, lowest price, and the most reliable.

Saxo Bank

This bank is also one of the top Forex Trading platforms in the market, not only does have competitive prices, but it comes with excellent trading platforms. It has excellent quality research and has reliable customer service. Meaning of the word traitor swears by this platform, Saxo bank offers the complete package which is worth being a customer for. Many Forex Traders will say that these are the most trustworthy platforms to work with when it comes to Forex Trading.

CMC Markets

Even though this platform has been office regulated, CMC Markets offers Traders one of the most comprehensive ranges of offerings with excellent pricing. It also has the next Generation trading platform, which is very Innovative and attracts a lot of younger Forex Traders into the platform. If you're looking for something that is futuristic and you can have fun with, then most definitely go for a CMC Markets. It has been known to be trustworthy amongst many Forex Traders, so this would be the right choice for you when it comes to starting your Forex Trading.

TD Ameritrade

This is perhaps one of her favorite platforms to trade in. Unfortunately, this is only available in the United States. However, what's nearly 80 currency pairs to trade alongside, and comes with a tremendous amount of trading tools this is no slouch. Moreover, the tools that provide you with the help you to succeed in Forex Trading. One of the safest platforms to work in and comes with excellent customer service. Highly recommended by many top Forex traders who are living in the United States, if you are living in the United States than we would highly recommend that you use this platform for your Forex needs.

Forex.com

This website has plenty of options for Forex Trading and many other Traders. Known to be beginner-friendly many people offer this platform when they're first starting, although we don't recommend that much if you're a beginner then you can most definitely start with this. But remember once you get a little bit better at four trading, you will eventually have to learn more about it and therefore this one be so useful anymore. Nonetheless, this is a great platform to start with when you're starting your forex trading.

CityIndex

The good thing is this broker caters to the client's needs. So if you do decide to work with them, he will feel more welcomed, and you will be able to manage it a little bit better as compared to other Forex Trading platform. This would be great for beginners as well, as it will help you with the tools you need to succeed in Forex Trading. They also offer many programs for Forex Traders, including a high-volume investor.

Xtb

This platform has been trusted by many, and several major Financial Centers have regulated it. Known to be one of the most excellent platform's trade in, it has competitive fitting experience and has fantastic customer service. If you're someone looking to be on top of your game, this platform would be an excellent idea for you. It offers fantastic tools that will help you to succeed in your forex trading needs.

Dukascopy

If you're looking for tools, under this platform offers many of them. More than any of the Forex Trading platforms mention to you in this chapter, not only that it has incredible market research and therefore can help you to succeed even more in Forex Trading. This would be our second option when it comes to starting your Forex Trading and to pick out a platform, and it is a mobile app that helps you to Forex trade. But also comes the desktop platform, the only problem with this platform is that they don't have too much to offer. Nonetheless, it is a great platform to get started with.

FXCM

If you're looking for a wide range of trading options, then this would be the best platform to go with. But this platform caters to more high-volume Traders, algorithmic raiders overall traders that appreciate tools and quality market research. If you're a beginner, then we would recommend that you stay away from this trading platform, however, once you've gotten your feet wet in Forex Trading then make sure to try the part for me as you will see great results from it.

Opening an Account

You must be excited about Forex trading. But, without learning the ways to open an account, how will you even trade? With online Forex trading, the excitement to trade Forex has increased immensely. However, to start trading Forex, you must find a broker, select a trading platform, and then open an account. But the part of opening an account is pretty easy. To open an account, you need certain things including name, email, address, contact number, account type, a password for the account, citizenship, date of birth, employment details, Tax ID, and a few more financial questions. The steps of opening an account will differ from one broker to another, yet the following are the general procedures to open an account:

Sometimes, you might have to fill the application with the details related to the trading experience.

Select the broker and check for the suitable and available account.

After completing the application, register with your username, and then you'll receive the credentials to your Forex trading account. Now, you'll have access to the broker's client portal.

And then, transfer the deposit funds through any of the possible payment methods to your trading account. But remember, you might have to bear charges as per the payment method.

Once the funding procedure is complete, you can then trade Forex. But, your broker will provide necessary guidance and ideas before you enter into live trading.

Once you complete these procedures, you are good to begin your journey. **But, are you wondering why you have to follow all these hectic rules and regulations?** Well, the Forex market wasn't filled with rules and regulations, but once the market allowed retail trading, the rules and regulations became compulsory. If the market wasn't strict, it would be easy for the market participants to gamble on the market. The factor of reliability will become questionable. Also, you will not find brokers who don't require these details. On the other hand, if you find brokers who don't ask these questions, then you have to think about opening an account. Well, an important thing about opening an account is risk disclosure. As a beginner, you are likely to be mindless about this factor, but remember, this is very important. If you are not aware of this, you might end up losing all your hard-earned money. Hence, you must make sure to read and understand everything before making a decision. I want to tell all new traders not to risk the amount that you are afraid to lose. Once you risk more than you are comfortable with, you have a constant fear. And in case one of the trades becomes a loss you will be depressed and frustrated. You need to be emotionally fit to become a profitable trader in the Forex market.

Trading Psychology

With a correct attitude towards Forex trading, you can be sure to achieve your goals. Here are a few suggestions that can help you develop the correct attitude and mindset for Forex trading and trading in general.

Be Patient

This is a virtue when it comes to Forex trading as it helps one cover everything at the right time and with the right state of mind. Patience can get you out of trouble as sometimes you might be forced to enter into a market hastily without understanding how it works. For beginners, patience is the key aspect as you get to understand the pros and cons of Forex trading. Patience also keeps you away from reacting out of a bad day in business and even making wrong choices and decisions that can cause big losses. As the adage goes, Patience pays, so take your time off a hectic day and trust the process.

Be Objective

In Forex trading, one is required to be objective and not trade with emotions. As stated earlier, a Forex trader should keep the eyes on the final product, that is, his financial goals. Being subjective or acting on emotions is disastrous for any business and learning to act by the book is key to a successful Forex trading career. This means that you should not also listen to people who claim to be Pros in the game and trust your trading patterns instead of sheepishly following the crowd.

This doesn't however mean that you should not trade on mass thinking but if you do, always keep in mind that the masses are not always right.

Be Disciplined

This ought to be a major aspect in every business and as earlier pointed out, discipline keeps one out of overreacting for a loss or a win. This cuts across happy and sad moments in business as both sides can affect the outcome if not subjected to some discipline. Being able to control yourself, to not overtrade or under trade and take just enough risks is a skill that can be learned by following procedures and sticking to the game-plan. Remember, you should never, ever, stake half your capital, risk all your profits or worse, trade with money you don't have or money you can't afford to lose.

Be Realistic

Just like any other business, one should be real and expect a particular profit according to the capital traded-in. Always remember that Forex trading is not like Lotto or betting where one can win a jackpot of a million dollars by stalking just a little money. It takes time to build up your skills, your knowledge and your confidence and secure good profits with Forex trading. Therefore, one should expect the right amount of returns on investment and what comes with it. By not giving up, being disciplined and patient, and doing your research, you might end up achieving your goals and reaching top-level in the Forex world. This mentality also helps one to limit the number and types of transactions or operations on a daily or weekly basis and to stay in the game even after losing a small percentage of the initial investment. This is a business opportunity just like any other. With all said and done, there are rules to abide by in order to reach your potential and most importantly realize your potential in terms of profit. Below are 12 rules that can help you achieve your goals in Forex Trading.

1 Trust The Process

Forex trading is a business and needs time and effort to grow and consolidate which means that there is more than just waiting for profits. Profit oriented businesses can end badly if the thresholds one has set are not met and the overall approach is not thoroughly planned. Any business is not only buying and selling as it involves huddles and logistics to make the whole institution work and doable. Some profit oriented forex traders tend to give up easily if they don't meet their target after a few operations or a short period of time. However, one can set a timeline and work towards meeting the set target without having to achieve a specific point which might turn to be the opposite. To achieve your goals, some points are process-oriented and help in reaching the high note in Forex trading and are outlined.

2 Outline Daily Activities

Day to day activities can only be achieved when put down on paper for a specific task in forex trading. Having in mind the right thing to do on a specific day is good as it helps avoiding distractions and other things that may get in the way on a business day.

This means that the more you know what you are doing on a busy day, you will not waste time doing other things that do not help achieve your goal and the needs you want to build your Forex trading skills.

3 Analyze The Market

As pointed out earlier, trading with emotions is bad for business as it does not go by the plans and strategy but with the reaction of business gone wrong or even a big win. Being greedy is so bad in Forex trading and it is advisable to analyze the market first before trying out Forex trading and giving a shot on the most promising patterns. When you play by the rules, you train the mind to follow the right procedures and even helps in becoming more discipline in Forex trading. Training the mind helps in a vulnerable situation which will make you hold on when there is a crisis.

4 Be Defensive

This is another important rule to follow in Forex trading for it is the core purpose of joining the business and what will keep you survive storms that will come your way in one way or the other. This simply means that you should not trade everything including your capital, defend your initial capital and aim at making profits. When you make a target and do not meet it, then at least you tried, but trading profusely just to meet the target with limited time is not good at all as it is an offensive approach. You should always protect your capital as it is the only thing keeping you in the business and one mistake can send you to factory reset, i.e; going back to the drawing board wondering when the rain started beating you.

5 Have A Trading Plan

Just like any other venture, Forex trading needs a business plan that has been tested to be working and giving impressive results. The plan involves things that you need to do from A-Z, this may include the rules of engagement, trading pattern, market analysis, and other key aspects that make the business run well. After making the trading plan, you can test it virtually to see if it will go well with the market and if it is good, then give it a green light and start the Forex trading. But make sure that you outline the plan as it is the backbone of the whole venture.

6 Know That Trading Is A Business

Forex trading is like a business and should be treated as such for one to get the best out of it by giving the attention it deserves. Other researches have talked about not comparing trading with job opportunities or hobby to be done on leisure time. This means that one should not expect a salary and works on getting profits and give attention and not only focusing on it when you are free. With this, a Forex trader will learn to prioritize Forex trading just like any other business.

7 Outline Risk

Make sure that you point out the risk you intend to get yourself into and do not give it too much until you are out of business. Do not risk an amount that you cannot afford, risking is only for the amount you are capable of and not anywhere near initial capital. Remember as said earlier, if you lose capital that means that you are out of business and you will not want that to happen to you.

Only risk an amount that you know if they go then you will not struggle with bringing back the business into living.

8 Use Technology

The modern era of inventions and innovations can be a plus in Forex trading as it helps improve the outcome of a venture. Technology has played a big role in Forex trading, thanks to innovators who come with new things every day to enhance the world in bringing people closer. With technology, one can trade anywhere in the world monitor charts using a computer or even mobile phones. This means that one can travel all over the world as well as working at the same time. This has been evident for bloggers and travel entrepreneurs who blog for a living and promote products online while they travel. This can be the same for Forex traders and it helps in even having a good time and relaxing the mind while working.

9 Have A Stop Loss

This is somehow similar to outlining risk but specifies the amount that one should be willing to lose in particular trading. In Forex trading, you should only lose what you afford and it is very important to outline the amount or percentage that one should only lose in trading. This also acts as a disciplined mode as it helps in controlling the mind and emotions not to surpass the limited amount of possible risk.

10 Focus On The Bigger Picture

What is the purpose of starting Forex trading? Can you make the business to be aligned in that direction? Are you getting some profits and losing sometimes? then you are on the right track heading to greatness in Forex trading. Business is not about just making profits but making impacts on a personal level and getting more skills. So what is your bigger picture? To have gained at least 10 per cent in the financial year 2020-2021? Having this in mind, then you can be sure of aiming in the right way as compared to only focusing on maximizing profits.

11 Keep Learning Markets

Forex trading is an ongoing process even after mastering markets and getting out of an amateur venture. One does not stop learning at anything and things keep changing in the Forex world this is important to keep an open mind in everything to do with business. Some of the skilled Forex traders can fall prey of crowd psychology and some markets are unpredictable making Forex trading a learning experience every time one is trading.

12 Be A Progressive Trader

Every Forex trader wants to earn profit as it is the main reason for venturing in Forex trading in the first place, but are you only profit-oriented the first day in the market or you are moving forward? Learning also can be a huge progress as it helps one avoid making similar mistakes and open ways for more profit in the future. A progressive trade is the one that celebrates every win either small or big as long as it is a victory.

Just like a child, you learn to sit then start crawling and in no time you start taking a few steps and eventually running. The same applies to Forex trading, you gradually move from one stage to the other and you cannot jump directly to only making profits. You either win or learn. After making a trading plan and testing it, one can join the trading business and encounter ups and downs as it shapes the ultimate goal of Forex trading. With this progress, one can be sure of securing a future in Forex trading full of experiences and lots of encounters that can prepare you to any hard hurdles that one might come across during your trading experience. So are you setting up your mind on winning and achieving your goals? If so I suggest you follow the suggestions outlined above and start winning small until you fully master the art of Forex trading and rejoice looking at your bank account after meeting your ultimate goals. Remember, Forex trading is not a walk in the park and you have to make the right choices.

Money Mistake to avoid

Now we'll turn our attention to giving some tips, tricks and advice on errors to avoid in order to ensure as much as possible that you have a successful time trading.

Avoid The Get Rich Quick Mentality

Any time that people get involved with trading or investing, the hope is always there that there's a possibility of the big winning trade. It does happen now and then. But quite frankly, it's a rare event. In many occasions, even experienced traders are guessing wrong and taking losses. It's important to approach Forex for what it really is. It's a business. It is not a gambling casino even though a lot of people treated that way so you need to come to your Forex business—and it is a business no matter if you do it part-time, or quit your job and devote your entire life to it—with the utmost seriousness. You wouldn't open a restaurant and recklessly buy 1 thousand pounds of lobster without seeing if customers were coming first. So, why would you approach Forex as if you were playing slots at the casino? Take it seriously and act as if it's a business because it really is. Again, it doesn't matter if you officially create a corporation to do your trades or not, it's still a business no matter what. That means you should approach things with care and avoid the get rich quick mentality. The fact is the get rich quick mentality never works anywhere. Unfortunately, I guess I could say I've been too strong in my assertion. It does work on rare occasions. It works well enough that it keeps the myth alive.

But if we took 100 Forex traders who have to get rich quick mentality, my bet is within 90 days, 95% of them would be completely broke.

Trade Small

You should always trade small and set small achievable goals for your trading. The first benefit to trading small is that this approach will help you avoid a margin call. Second, it will also help you set profit goals that are small and achievable. That will help you stay in business longer.Simply put, you will start gaining confidence and learning how to trade effectively if you get some trades that make $50 profits, rather than shooting for a couple of trades that would make thousands of dollars in one shot, but and up making you completely broke. Again, treat your trading like a real business. If you were opening a business, chances are you would start looking for slow and steady improvements and you certainly would not hope to get rich quick..Let's get specific. Trading small means never trading standard lots. Even if you have enough cash to open an account such that you could trade standard lots, I highly recommend that you stay away from them. The large amount of capital involved and margin that would be used could just get you into a lot of financial trouble. For beginners, no matter how much money you are able to devote to your trading, I recommend that you start with micro lots. Take some time and learn how to trade with the small lots and start building your business earnings small profits at a time. Trading only with micro lots will help in force discipline and help you avoid getting into trouble. Make a commitment only to use micros for the first 60 days. After that, if you have been having decent success, consider trading a mini lot.

You should be extremely cautious for the first 90 days in general.

Be Careful With Leverage

Obviously, it's extremely beneficial. It allows you to enter and trades that would otherwise not be possible. On the other hand, the temptation is there to use all your leverage in the hopes of making it big on one or two trades. You need to avoid using up all your leverage. Remember that you can have a margin call and get yourself into big trouble if your trades go bad. And it's important to remember there's a high probability that some of your trades are going to go bad no matter how carefully you do all your analysis.

Not Using A Demo Account

A big mistake the beginners make, is jumping in too quickly. There is a reason that most broker-dealers provide demos or simulated accounts. If you don't have a clue what that reason is, let's go ahead and stated here. Brokers provide demo accounts because Forex is a high-risk trading activity. It can definitely be something that provides a lot of rewards and it does for large numbers of traders. But there is a substantial risk of losing your capital. Many beginners are impatient hoping to make money right away. That's certainly understandable, but you don't want to fall into that trap. Take 30 days to practice with a demo account. This will provide several advantages. Trading on Forex is different than trading on the stock market. Using the demo account, you can become familiar with all the nuances of Forex trading. This includes everything from studying the charts, to placing your orders and, most importantly,understanding both pips and margin.

The fact that there is so much leverage available means you need to learn how to use it responsibly.

You need to know how to experience going through the process and reading the available margin and so forth on your trading platform while you are actually trying to execute trades. A demo account let you do this without risking real capital. It is true that it's not a perfect simulation. The biggest argument against demo accounts is that they don't incorporate the emotion that comes with trading and real money. As we all know, it's those emotions, including panic, fear and greed, that lead to bad decisions. However, in my opinion, that is a weak argument against using demo accounts. The proper way to approach it is to use a demo account for 30 days and then spend 60 to 90 days doing nothing but trading micro lots. Don't worry, as your micro trading lots you can increase the number of your trades and earn profits. While I know you're anxious to get started, keeping yourself from losing all your money is a good reason to practice for 30 days before doing it for real.

Failing To Check Multiple Indicators

There is also a temptation to get into trades quickly just on a gut level hunch. You need to avoid this approach at all costs. Some beginners will start learning about candlesticks and then when they first start trading, they will recognize a pattern on a chart. Then in the midst of the excitement, they will enter a large trade based on what they saw. And then they will end up on the losing end of a trade. Some people are even worse and they don't even look at the candlesticks.

Instead, they just look at the trend and think they better get in on it and they got all anxious about doing so. That means first checking the candlesticks and then confirming at least with the moving average before entering or exiting a position. You should also have the RSI handy and you may or may not want to use Bollinger bands.

Use Stop Loss And Take Profit Orders

Well, I hate to repeat myself yet again, but this point is extremely important. I am emphasizing it over and over because it's one of the tools that you can use in order to protect yourself from heavy losses. One of the ways that you can get out of having to worry about margin calls and running out of money is to put stop-loss orders every time you trade. This will require studying the charts more carefully. You need to have a very clear idea where you want to get out of the trade, if it doesn't go in the direction you hoped. But if you have a stop-loss order in place, then you can avoid the problem of having your account just go down the toilet. Secondly, although the temptation is always there to look for as many profits as possible, in most cases, you should opt to set a take profit order when you make your trade. That way you set as we said, distinct boundaries which will ensure that you make some profit without taking too much risk. The problem with doing it manually is that excitement and greed will put you in a position where are you miss the boat entirely. What inevitably happens, is people get too excited hoping to earn more profits and they stay in the trade too long. The Forex market changes very fast and so what eventually happens is people that stay into long inevitably and up with a loss. Or at the very least they end up missing out on profits.

There is one exception to this point. There are some times when there is a distinct and relatively long-term upward trend. If you find yourself, by doing the analysis and determining that such an upward trend is here, that might be an exception to the rule. In that case you want to try to ride the trend and maximize your profits.

Remember Price Changes Are In Pips

Beginners often make the mistake of forgetting about pips. If you have trouble with pips and converting them to actual money, go back and review the examples we provided. Remember that pips play a central role in price changes, you need to know your dollar value per pip in order to keep tabs on your profit and losses. This is also important for knowing the right stop loss and take profit orders to execute.

Don't Try Too Many Strategies Or Trading Styles At Once

When you are a beginning Forex trader, it can be tempting to try everything under the sun. That can be too much for a lot of people. The most advisable thing to do is to stick with one strategy so don't try scalping and being a position trader at the same time. The shorter the time frame for your trades, the more time and energy, you have to put into each trade. Scalping and day trading are activities that would require full-time devotion. They are also high-pressure and that can help enhance emotions involved in the trades. For that reason, I don't really recommend those styles or strategies for beginners. In my opinion and to be honest it's mine alone, I think position trading is also too much for a beginner. It requires too much patience.

Perhaps the best strategy to use when you're beginning Forex trading is to become a swing trader. It's a nice middle ground, in between the most extremely active trading styles and something that is going to try people's patience such as position trading. When you do swing trading, you can do time periods longer than a day certainly, but as long or short as you need to meet your goals otherwise. Swing trading also takes off some of the pressure. And it gives you more time to think and react. This does not mean that you can't become a scalper or day trader at some future date. What I am advising is that you gain some experience using more relaxed trading styles before taking that path. And believe me, swing trading is going to be challenging enough.

Market Expectations

Life as a Forex trader can sometimes get lonely. After all, this is the kind of career where you are completely on your own. You enjoy your profits alone, but you also suffer losses on your own. There is no one in the Forex market whom you can depend on to comfort you. Therefore, it is also good if you connect with like-minded people. Feel free to make friends with other traders. After all, you are all players in the market who want the same thing. The good thing is that you are not competing with one another. In fact, you can even help one another by sharing information, insights, and strategies. Thanks to the Internet, it is very easy to find and connect with people who are also interested in Forex trading. You simply have to join an online group or forum on Forex trading. You can do this quickly with just a few clicks of a mouse. You can then make a public post or even send a private message to any member of the group/forum.

If you have a neighbor or friend who also likes trading currencies, then you can invite him out for a coffee one of these days. Connecting with like-minded people is not just a way to learn but it can also inspire you to become a better trader.

- **Have fun**

Forex trading is fun. This is a fact. In fact, many traders get to enjoy this kind of life that they still continue to learn it despite their losses. It is also not uncommon to find traders, especially beginners, who spend their whole day just learning about Forex trading. Like gambling in a casino, trading currencies can also be very addicting, especially if you are making a nice profit from it.

Learn to have fun and enjoy the journey. Sometimes taking things too seriously can ruin the experience and even make you less effective. In your life as a trader, you will definitely make some mistakes from time to time. You will experience losing money from what otherwise would have been a profitable trade if only you knew better. Do not get too stressed. The important thing is for you to learn as much as you can from every mistake. Take it easy, but remember to learn from the experience. Making mistakes is part of the learning process. Of course, you should try to minimize them as much as possible. Learn and have fun.

Risk Management

Risks do occur in every sphere of life. However, when it comes to trading in Forex securities, these risks, more so, financial risks are enhanced. This is due to the volatility of the foreign exchange currencies.

Nature of Forex risk

Forex risk (currency risk, FX risk or exchange rate risk) is a risk (financial) that prevails when a financial transaction is monetized in a foreign currency. When it comes to multinationals, Forex risk occurs when one or several of its subsidiaries maintain financial records and statements in currencies other than those of the parent entity. When it comes to a multinational, there is a risk that there could be negative movements in foreign currency of the subsidiary entities in relation to the domestic currency of the parent entity prior to the report being compiled. International traders are also exposed to this risk.

Types of Forex risks

There are many types of Forex risks. Nonetheless, the following are the major types of Forex risk: - **Transaction risk –** This occurs where a firm has cash commitments whose values are subject to unforeseeable changes in exchange rate due to a contract being considered in foreign currency. The cash commitments may include account receivables and account payables.

- **Economic risk** – A firm is exposed to economic risk when its market value is susceptible to unanticipated changes in forex rate. This may affect the firm's share value, present and future values of cash flows, firm's market position and ultimately firm's overall value.

- **Translation risk** – Translation risk affects mainly multinational firms. Thus, a firm's translation risk is the susceptibility of its financial statements and reports to Forex changes. This happens when a parent firm has to prepare consolidated statements, including those of its foreign subsidiaries. This largely affects the firms reported income. This also affects its stock value in the securities market.

- **Contingent risk** – Contingent risks occurs when a firm engages in foreign contracts thus resulting in foreign-denominated obligations. Such foreign contracts may include bidding for foreign projects, commitments to foreign direct investment (for example, investing in foreign subsidiaries), and settling legal disputes involving foreign entities.

Trading Mindset

We will talk about what you should be doing, to make sure that you are not failing in your endeavors to start your Forex trading journey without making it too hard on yourself. Will show you what you could be doing to make Forex trading your lifestyle and to not only help you to start your trading journey but to stay on track. These daily patterns will help you not to fail when trading, and we understand that you might fail a couple of times in anything you do, and it is understandable to do so. Many successful people have followed these habits, to get optimal results in all of their aspects of life, whether it be job-related or anything else. Make sure you start implementing all of these habits after you are done reading this book as it will help you to make Forex trading much easier for you. The reason why this chapter might sound philosophical is that the only way you will see success with Forex trading is if you do it consistently.

Plan your day ahead

Planning your day ahead of time is crucial, not only does planning out your day help you be more prepared for your day moving forward, but it will also help you to become more aware of the things you shouldn't be doing, hence wasting your time. Moreover, planning your day will truly help you with making the most out of your time, that being said we will talk about two things 1. Benefits of planning out your day 2. How to go about planning out your day. So without further ado, let us dive into the benefits of planning out your day.

It will help you prioritize:

Yes, planning out your day will help you prioritize a lot of things in your day to day life. You can allow time limits to the things you want to work on the most to least, for example, if you're going to write your book and you are super serious about it. Then you need a specific time limit every day in which you work on a task wholeheartedly without any worries of other things until the time is up. Then you move on to the next job in line, so when you schedule out your whole day, and you give yourself time limits, then you can prioritize your entire day. The same thing goes for your trading, make sure you allocate time for trading, which will allow you to be more focused on your research, hence making you more successful.

Summarize your normal day:

Now, before we start getting into planning out your whole day ahead, you need to realize that to plan your entire day, you need to know precisely what you are doing that day. Which means you need to write down every single thing you do on a typical day and write down the time you start and end, it needs to be detailed in terms of how long does it take for your transportation to get to work, etc.

Now after you have figured out your whole day, you can decide how to prioritize your day moving on could be cutting out a task that you don't require or shortening your time for a job that doesn't need that much time. After you have your priorities for the day, you can add pleasurable tasks into your day like hanging out with your friends, etc.

Arrange your day It is crucial that you arrange your day correctly, so the best way to organize your day is to make sure you get all your essential stuff done earlier in the day when your mind is fresh. After that's done, you can have some time for yourself to relax and do whatever it is that you want. But make sure you get all the things that need to be done before you can move on to free time for yourself. Another thing that will help you is to set time limits on each task, and once you start setting time limits, you will be more likely to get the job done.

Remove all the fluff

So, what I mean by that is remove all the things that are holding you back from achieving your goals. Make sure you remove all of the things that are holding you back from getting the things that you need to be doing. If you have time for the fluff, do it if not, then work on your priorities first. In conclusion, planning out your day will help you tremendously! Make sure you plan out your day every day to ensure successful and accomplished days.

Cut out negative people

This task might be the hardest to do, but it is quite essential, see the people who you are around are the people who will create your personality. So if you are around negative people, you will develop adverse circumstances for yourself, so if you are around people who are not upbeat about life and find everything wrong and never see the good in anyone, you need to cut them out and be around people who are happy and ready for what life has to offer.

Now I get it, some cynical people can be your family members, and you can't cut them out, the ideal thing to do is 1. Make them understand what they are doing wrong 2. Show them how they can change their life. And if they still want to remain the same, then keep your distance. In conclusion, It is essential that you are in a grateful "vibe" as it will not only help you with your mental and physical health, but it will also help you attract better people and better circumstances.

Now that we have covered the part of being grateful, and how it can help you with your day to day life and eating habits. Let us give you some concrete ideas on how to change the way you live your experience and to make it better.

Stop multitasking

I think we are all guilty of this at a time, and if are multitasking right now, I need you to stop. Now multitasking could be a lot of things, and it could be as small as cooking and texting at the same time, or it could be as big as working on two projects at the same time. Studies are showing how multitasking can reduce your quality of work, which something you don't want to do if your goal is to get the best result out of the thing that you are doing. That being said, there are a lot more reasons as to why you shouldn't be multitasking, so without further ado, lets get into the primary reasons why multitasking can be harmful.

You're not as productive.

Believe it or not, you tend to be a lot less productive when you are multitasking. When you go from one project to another or anything else for that matter, you don't put all your effort into your work. You are always worried about the project that you will be moving into next. So moving back and forth from one project to another will affect your productivity if you want to get the most out of your work you need to be focused on one thing at a time and make sure you get it done to the best of your abilities. Plus, you are more likely to make mistakes, which will not help you work at the best of your ability.

You become slower at your work.

When you are multitasking, chances are you will end up being slower at completing your projects. You would be in a better position if you were to focus on one project at a time instead of going back and forth, which of course helps you complete them faster. So the thing that enables you to be faster at your projects when you're not multitasking is the mindset, we often don't realize how much mindset comes into play. When you are going back and forth from one project to another, you are in a different mental state going into another project which takes time to build and break. So by the time you have managed to get into the mindset of project A you are already moving into project B, it is always best that you devote your time and energy one project at a time if you want it to doe did an at a faster pace.

Set yourself a goal (time, quality, etc.)

All in all, multitasking will do you no good. It will only make you slower at your work and make you less productive. Making sure you stop multitasking is essential, as it will only help you live a better life. One thing to remember from this chapter is to put all your energy at one thing at a time, and this will yield you a lot better projects or anything that you are working towards to be great. If you want to be more successful and live a better life, you need to make sure your projects are quality as I can't stress this point enough. You are probably reading this book because you want to get better at living your life or achieve goals which you haven't yet. One of the reasons why you are not living the life that you want or haven't reached your goal could be a lot of things but, one of the items could be the quality of your work which could be taking a hit because of your multitasking. So review yourself, and find out why you haven't achieved your goal and why you are not living the life that you want. Then if you happen to stumble upon multitasking being the limiting factor or the quality of your work, I want you to stop multitasking and start working on one project at a time while giving it your full attention. What you will notice is that your work will have a higher quality and will be completed in a quicker amount of time following the steps listed above, which will change your life and help you achieve your life goals in a better more efficient way. Now that we have talked about some action items in regards to making forex trading more of a lifestyle by changing the way you set up your day.

Let us talk about some of the lifestyle changes you need to make, in regards to making trading easier for you.

Get more sleep

It is essential that you start getting your 8 hours of sleep. Many people don't know this but, even if your eating is perfect but you still aren't getting the sleep chances are you are not going to see the changes. Getting your 8 hours of sleep helps you a lot. When you get the right amount of deep sleep, you will see results such as better recovery and better mental health. It is essential that you get your full 8 hours of sleep if you don't, then your Forex trading endeavors might go to vain. Not only that, if you don't get enough sleep, the chances of you staying awake the next morning will drop down tremendously. You will be a lot sleepier the days you don't get your full sleep. Keep that in mind moving on, and as always make sure to get your total 8 hours of sleep.

Physical activity

It is very crucial for you to take part in physical activities, for a straightforward reason it will help you to assist your motivation to trade. The same thing as getting proper sleep, the role of you being physically active will give you a great balance of you being energized and motivated throughout the day. Many people don't know this, but being physically active can help you to stay more motivated. There have been many studies backing these claims up, that being said, let's talk about some of the benefits which might come along with you following a working out plan.

Regular exercising changes your brain

No, regular exercises does not change the way your brain is shaped by any means if that's what you're thinking. But what it will help with, is better memory and better-thinking skills. If you where to do your research, you will find that out for yourself, how big of a role regular exercising plays when it comes to brain functions. Make sure you start implementing this physical activity, it will only help you get better at your trading skills and to see better results out of it.

By now you can see the benefits of exercising, not only does regular exercising help you stay healthy physically, but it also enables you to optimize your mind and helps you with better brain function which will allow you to work for an extended period at any given task.

Improves your mood

This is one of the most significant differences you will notice once you start working on your health is that your mood will stay elevated through the day! Which is a great thing to have as you will be able to get more things done and be more successful. See when you workout you release a chemical called dopamine, which is a feel-good hormone and of course working out will help you become less stressed.

Improves physical health

Yes, this is one of the most salient points to bring up but let's discuss it anyway. Once you start to implement healthy habits to your day you will become more physically fit, which will not only give you more energy through the day, it will also help you keep up with things like your daily chores and not get tired so quickly. You will see a difference in the quality of your life and your work ethic once you start to implement daily health habits and become more physically healthy.

Helps boost your immune system

This ties into improved physical health, but working out will boost your immune system and lower your risk of diseases like diabetes, hypertension, etc. Once you have a boost in your immune system, you will be less likely to get even the common flu. I know of someone who hasn't gotten flu in fifteen years simply because he started to live a healthy life, now I am not saying that you will see the same results but staying healthy will definitely help you with boosting your immune system which will help you not get sick so often and enjoy some quality time with your family and get more stuff done.

Now that we have discussed how staying in shape can help you live a better life, we will now move on to the ways you can help yourself live a healthier life.

Start easy

Now, if you have never worked out in your life, you need to realize that you won't be going hard at the gym as Arnold Schwarzenegger did in his hay days. So don't push yourself too much in the gym because you are not ready for it, and you might lose motivation. So if you are starting off getting in shape perhaps light jogs, some resistance training couple times a week to get the blood moving. But make sure you get up to the point where you are working out at least three hours a week to see some health benefits. Start once a week then twice, and so on. After reading this chapter, many might be thinking that this is more of a self-help book than it is Forex trading. The Truth is that we want you to understand how to live a better life by changing the habits that you are currently following. Doing Forex trading and making it a lifestyle is a lot more work than you think it is. For you to make it easy, you need to understand that you need to change your habits to be successful at Forex trading, which means you need to change the way you move the way you think and the way you perform. This chapter gives you a clear idea on how to start living a better life by changing up your habits, once you do change your practices you will notice that Forex trading as a whole will be straightforward for you. The reason why it will be straightforward for you is that you will change the way you move and the change the way you live your life in general. Changing the way you live your life will not only help you get better results, but it will also help you to make Forex trading a lifestyle, many people confuse income source as not being a part of a lifestyle, and it is something that they're supporting to better their health.

But the Truth is that when they're working on trading, they don't realize that it needs to be a lifestyle for it to be a health benefit, if you want to be healthier then you need to make sure that you're taking care of your health 24/7 365 days a year.

Which means you need to make this a lifestyle, and for you to make this a lifestyle, we need to understand some self-help techniques to keep it sustained for a more extended period. Which is why this chapter being more self-help oriented, we wanted to make sure that this book is different from any other books that you've read when it comes to starting your Forex trading journey. The way we're going to be delivering it is by showing you how to change your lifestyle for the better instead of the worst.

Conclusion

Many people are turning to trade in order to generate their income, invest in their future, or simply give themselves extra cash for the month. Whatever your reason is for getting into trading, you learned four different types of trading strategies within the contents of this book. First, you learned positions trading, which allows you to hold your position for months to a year. Second, you learned about swing trading, which focuses on the position you hold for a few days to a couple of weeks. Third, you were given some information on day trading, which focuses on buying and selling all your trades in one day and finally learned about scalping trading, which is often called the minute strategy as you hold a position only for a few seconds to a minute or two.

Now you not only understand these four strategies better, but you also understand the basics of forex trading. You also understand the basic risks involved, have the know-how needed to achieve the winning mindset, know how to search for a trusted broker, and how to get a start and gain a profit.

To become a successful trader, you need to continue your education, studying in more detail the type of strategy you want to focus on. This means you have to read more books, research online, join at least one online community and begin talking to a mentor or to more experienced traders who are willing to help and guide you. Even though the market is competitive, people still want to help one another and make sure they have the best possible experience.

Above all, some of the most important steps to remember are the following: do your research, set your daily schedule, have patience, have the right mindset, and be self-disciplined. Also make sure you are paying attention to what the charts show you. You will want to note the candlestick charts, so you can understand if the price in moving in an upward or downward trend. You will also want to look at the trend charts, which will give you a variety of colored lines to explain how well the currencies are performing and if they would be a good fit for you. Taking into consideration all these different factors, you will become a successful trader no matter what strategy you decide to use. One of the biggest parts of becoming successful is believing you can be successful. By following the tips and tricks outlined in this book, you will be able to reach the goal you have set or are about to set for yourself.

Through all the information you have read in this book, you will be able to apply your favorite forex trading strategy. Through practice, you will be able to master your preferred strategy which will allow you to gain bigger profits. It doesn't matter which strategy you decide to use. What matters is that you are confident in your abilities and remain consistent with your strategy.

There are many websites online that offer you the possibility to try out Forex trading by using the trading platform in DEMO mode BEFORE you even start trading with real money, and such websites will have to become an integral part of your study as you explore this field of trade.

Introduction Swing Trading

Swing trading is an exciting opportunity for small and individual investors to make an income on the stock market. In fact, swing trading is a general technique that can be used to earn income from stocks, commodities, and even on Forex. You can think of swing trading as a middle ground between long term investing and day trading. We will explore the similarities and differences along with specific details in the book, but, for now, you can think of swing trading as day trading but over longer time frames and with far less risk. Rather than trying to make money off of your trades in the matter of a few hours, with swing trading your goal is to make money off changing share prices over time frames ranging from days to many weeks. A swing trader doesn't need to sit at his computer watching the stock markets all day long, although you certainly can if that is an option for you and you like doing it. Swing traders can also start small and grow their business over time. Day trading involves lots of upfront costs instead. The word "business" should catch your eye. In short, swing trading is a business. Rather than building a long-term retirement account, swing trading is all about earning profits in the short term. While substantial profits are possible, it's not a get-rich-quick scheme and although it can be done on a part-time basis, we want you to start thinking of swing trading as a business from this point forward. The goal is to earn profits, and you can use those profits as ordinary income if you like or reinvest them to build your retirement account or some combination of the two.

That is entirely up to you. But keep in mind one thing: very few people are going to make a million bucks in their first year and go right into retirement.

That said, swing trading can be a very lucrative way to make a living, and if you are interested in business and finance, it can be a lot of fun! In order to get there, you are going to have to study and become an expert in the field. The journey can start with this book. Let's get started!

How Swing Trading Works

It is a style of trading that attempts to catch benefits a securities trading inside one to four days of the period. It is likewise named as a momentary pattern following trading s. Investopedia Explains Swing Trading: To spot circumstances in which a stock or item has super potential to make developments in a shorter period outline, the dealer or the financial specialist must act carefully and quickly. This is predominantly utilized by the home brokers and the informal investors. Huge foundations for the most part trading measure that are too huge to move all through products quickly. In addition, the merchant or the financial specialist is fit for workaholic behavior the momentary stock developments and that likewise with no challenge with the huge and effective speculators. Swing merchants generally utilize specialized examination to view the stocks and items which are accessible in momentary value motivation. Such brokers are not intrigued by the crucial estimations of the offers, rather, are keen on realizing the value patterns and different examples. For what reason is Swing Trading the Preferred Approach? Swing trading is the best proficient methodology towards profiting and money in the entire financial trading. Continuously see the cost from where the stock diagrams start and where it closes. This is the situation of the customary financial specialist and the merchant. Notwithstanding sitting tight for a really long time periods for any stock or product to move in the normal course, you ought to duplicate your advantages simultaneously and that likewise with both long and short trading s.

About $10,000 or more can be earned on the off chance that you trading the all over swings in contrast with the purchasing and holding the stock. In addition, swing trading is superior to anything the day trading in light of the fact that it is compelling than the day trading style, and even the cost related the business set up is additionally low on the grounds that the commissions are not rendered day by day. The swing dealers likewise have the chance to share among the more critical pieces of the value developments.

Swing Trading May be Right for you if:

If any of the accompanying explanations portray your trading yields,

Swing trading may demonstrate to be directly for you: You are disappointed with the low back up qualities on the purchase and-hold ventures and imagine that there is another better way. Swing trading will be all the more stuffing for you on the off chance that you won't keep a track on the business sectors entire day. Here and there you may feel dull and depleted, however you should work in a similar issue. It is certainly for you on the off chance that you have had the option to realize that you can profit just when you will apply your trading s inverse bearings for all your initial trading s of the stocks and wares. What Are Its Benefits The way toward swing trading has turned into a viral stock trading procedure utilized by numerous brokers over the market.

This style of trading has demonstrated to be exceptionally effective for some dedicated stocks and Forex merchants.

Customarily swing trading has been characterized as a progressively theoretical system as the positions are typically purchased and held for the merchant's foreordained time period. These time allotments could go somewhere in the range of two days to a couple of months. The objective of the swing broker is to recognize the pattern either up or down and place their trading s the most favorable position. From that point, the dealer will ride the heading to what they decide as the depletion point and sell for a benefit. Regularly, swing brokers will use a wide range of specialized markers that will enable them to have a progressively worthwhile likelihood when making their trading s. Shorter-term brokers don't really will in general swing trading as they incline toward holding positions for the duration of the day and practicing them before the end of the market. Swing trading methodology uses time, and it is this time is the obstacle factor for a long-time broker. Regularly there is an excessive amount of hazard engaged with the end of the market and that a broker won't acknowledge this hazard. The qualification of swing trading is a wide subject in that it has various impacts from a huge number of various trading procedures. These trading techniques are interesting and have their separate hazard profiles. Swing trading can be a fantastic route for a market member to improve their specialized examination abilities further while enabling them to give more consideration to the crucial side of trading. Numerous fruitful swing merchants have been known to utilize a Bollinger band procedure as a device to help them in entering and leaving positions. Obviously, for a swing broker to be fruitful at the arrangement, they should have a high fitness for deciding the present market pattern and setting their situations by that pattern.

It makes a swing merchant note great to put a short post with the arrangement of holding for an all-inclusive period in a market that is drifting upwards. The general subject here is that the objective of the dealers ought to be to build their likelihood of progress while restricting or disposing of hazard. The swing dealer's most noticeably terrible foe is that of a sideways or in a functioning business sector. Sideways value activity will stop a swing broker cold in their tracks as there is no common pattern to key off of.

The Basics Of Swing Trading.

Now, it is time to move on and get to some of the basics about doing an actual swing trade. We are going to take a look at some of the steps that you need to take in order to enter the market, the types of positions that you can choose to take, and even how to take each of the positions that you choose. This will help you to get set up when it is time to do that first trade with this kind of trading strategy!

Choosing to Buy Long or Sell Short

The price of a stock is going to do one of three things at a given time. It will either go down, go up, or it will move sideways. When you enter into the market as a swing trader, you are expecting that the stock is going to either go up or it will go down. If you think that the stock will see an increase in its price, then they will purchase the stock.

This move is going to be considered "going long" or having a "long position" in that stock. For example, if you are long 100 shares of Facebook Inc., it means that you purchased 100 shares of this company and you are making the prediction that you will be able to sell them at a higher price later on and earn a nice profit.

That one is pretty easy to understand, but what if you are looking at a stock and you expect that the price is going to decrease? When this situation occurs, you can choose to borrow shares and then later sell them with the expectation that you will purchase them back at a lower price and make a profit later on. At this point, you may be wondering how it is possible for you to sell shares that you don't own or that you don't hold in your own account?

This is pretty simple. Brokerages have a mechanism that will allow a trader to borrow the shares. When you end up selling shares that you don't actually own, it means that you are "going short" or "being short' on a stock. When a trader says that they are short on a stock, it means that they borrowed shares from the broker and then sold them with the expectations that the price will drop, and they will be able to replace those shares by purchasing them later at a lower price.

When you are setting up an account to trade, you will probably need to take the time to fill out some additional forms with the broker so that you can take this short position with a stock. You should also have an idea that this option can be riskier compared to just going long or purchasing a stock, so you must be actively there to manage the position.

Short selling can be an important tool for you as a swing trader because the prices of the stocks are usually going to drop much faster than they will go up. It is a good rule of thumb to say that stocks are going to fall three times faster than they rise. This is often because of the human psyche; the fear of loss is more powerful than the desire for a gain.

When the stock starts to move down, shareholders are going to fear that they will have to lose their profits or gains, and they move to sell that quickly. This selling activity is going to feed into more selling as shareholders continue to take the profits and traders start to shorten. This additional shorting activity adds to the downward pressure that is there on the price. This sends the price of the stock into a strong decline, which means that short sellers are able to make a good amount of profits while long traders and other investors are going to enter panic mode and may try to dump their shares to protect themselves.

Knowing this information can make it easier to do the trades that you want. It can help you to figure out which position you would like to enter based on how the market or that particular stock is doing at the time. This also shows you that it is possible to get into the market and make profits, no matter which direction you think the market is heading.

How to Enter a Trade

If you are brand new to trading, you are probably curious about how you would sell or purchase a security. Any time that the market is open, there are going to be two prices for any security that can be traded. There will be the bid price and the ask price. The bid price is what buying or purchasing traders are offering to pay for that stock right then. The ask price, on the other hand, is the price that traders want in order to sell that security.

You will quickly notice that the bid price is always going to be a bit lower simply because the buyers want to pay less, and the asking price is always going to be higher because sellers want more for their holdings. The difference between these two prices is known as the spread. The spreads that are found will vary for each stock, and they can even change throughout the day. If a stock doesn't have a ton of buyers and sellers, then there could be a bigger spread. When there are more buyers and sellers, then the spread between these two prices will be much lower. As a swing trader, when you are ready to enter into a position, you are going to have two choices. You can either go in or pay the price that the seller is asking for right away or you can place a bid that is at or below the bid price. Paying the asking price immediately can be beneficial because it ensures that the purchase transaction is completed or filled but may mean that you will pay more for it. When a trader places a bit at or below the current bid price, they may be able to make the purchase at a lower price. But, there is the risk that no seller will want to sell for the lower price, and the order may not get filled.

When you are ready to get started with a trade, you will simply need to pick out your trading platform, pick out a stock, and then decide whether you want to pay the asking price or wait and see if you can get it for the bid price. Then, you can enter into the trade and complete the rest of your strategy.

Investment and Margin Accounts

There are two types of accounts that you can choose to open in order to trade stocks. The two main options include the margin account and the investment account. With a margin account, you can borrow against the capital that you have placed in your account. The investment account, on the other hand, will allow you to buy up to the dollar value you hold in that account. You are not able to spend more than what you have put in that account at a time. When you decide to open up a margin account, you may be able to borrow money from the investment or brokerage firm to help pay for some of your investment. This is a process that is known as buying on margin. This can provide you with some advantages of purchasing more shares that you would be able to afford if you just used the capital in your account, and it can help you leverage to get more profits with your money. However, there is a catch with this one in the form of more risks. When you borrow the money to do your investments, there will come a point when you must pay the loan back. If you earn the profits that you think you will, it is easy to pay this back. But, if you lose out and make the wrong predictions, you are going to have to find other ways to pay the money back. Making investments with leverage can magnify the percentage losses on your money.

As a beginner, you should stick with a regular investment account. Trading on margin can increase the amount of risk that you are taking on in your trades. This may be tempting because it can increase your potential profits, but there is a lot more risk that comes with it as well. You will do much better going with an investment account instead. This way, you can just pull out the money that you are comfortable with rather than hoping that you make a good prediction in the beginning when you are learning.

Picking out a Broker

During this process, we also need to take some time to discuss picking out a broker. If you have already gotten into other forms of trading in the past, then you can simply work with the same broker that you already have. But, if you are getting into trading and this is the first one you have done before, then you will need to search to find the right broker for you. There are many different brokers out there, and many of them can assist you with swing trading. The biggest thing that you will want to look at is the commissions and fees that each broker assesses against you. Since swing trading times are relatively short and you will enter into and out of trades within a few weeks at most with each trade, you want to make sure that the profits you make aren't eaten up by the commissions to your broker. There are different methods that the broker can use to come up with their fees. Some will charge a fixed rate for the whole year. This often works well for long-term trades and probably won't be an option available to you since you will do more trades. The two options that you will most likely deal with include a fee for each trade or a fee based on how much profit you earn.

If you can, find a broker who will earn a fee based on your profits. This way, you are not charged a ton if you do a bunch of trades during that time. If you earn a good profit, you will have to pay a bit more because of the percentage. If you earn less on one of your trades, then you won't have to pay the broker as much as you did before. Before you enter into any trade, make sure that you discuss the fees with your broker. They should be able to outline their fees and can discuss with you where your money will go when you work with them. This can help you to get a good idea of how much you will spend based on how much you earn, how many trades you decide to enter into, and more. Get the commissions and fees in writing, along with any other agreements that you and the broker and their firm agree to in order to protect you.

Tools And Platforms

Normally, foreign exchange involves selling and purchasing of different currencies across the world. The number of participants in this market is very large therefore the liquidity is very high. The most unique aspect of the forex trade is that individual traders can compete against large institutions such as hedge funds and commercial banks; all one needs to do is to select the right account and set it up. There are different types of accounts but the traders have three main options namely mini accounts, standard accounts, and managed accounts. Each account has its own advantages and disadvantages. The type of account that one opts for depends on factors such as the size of initial capital, risk tolerance levels, and the hours one has to analyze the charts either daily or at different intervals.

Mini Trading Accounts

Simply put, a mini account is one that allows the trader to transact using mini lots. For most brokerage firms, one mini lot equals to 10,000 units. That is equal to 1/10 of a standard account. Brokerage firms offer mini lots to attract new traders who are still hesitant to trade with bigger accounts or those who do not have the investment funds required. The advantages of Mini accounts include low risk, low capital required and flexibility. The trader can trade in increments of 10,000 units therefore if he or she is inexperienced, he or she does not have to worry about blowing through their account and capital. Experienced traders can use the mini accounts to test new strategies without excessive risk. A mini account can be opened with as little as $100, $250 or $500 and the leverage can go up to 400:1. A risk management plan is the key to successful trading and in the case of selecting lots; a trader can minimize the risk by buying a number of mini lots to minimize risk. Remember that one standard lot is equal to about 10 mini lots and diversification reduces risk. The main disadvantage of mini accounts is low reward. A lower risk translates to a lower reward. A mini lot account can only produce $1 per pip movement if it is trading 10000 lots. In a standard account, one pip movement equals to $10.

A subset of the mini account is the micro account which is offered by some online broker. This account has very little risk and also very little reward. The trade is 1000 base currency units and one pip movement earns or loses 10 cents. These accounts are best suited for traders who have very little knowledge about forex trade and one can open using as little as 25 dollars.

Standard Trading Accounts

The standard trading accounts are the most common for traders especially the experienced ones. These accounts give a trader access to lots of currency worth 100,000 units each. This, however, does not mean that a trader has to put $100,000 in the account as capital so as to trade. The rules of leverage and margin mean that all a trader need is $1000 to have a margin account. The main advantage of this account is the large reward that one might reap with the right strategy and predictions. One pip movement earns $ 10. Again, individuals who own such accounts get better services and perks because of the upfront capital invested in the account.

The disadvantages include high initial capital and potential for loss. The kind of capital required to set up a standard account can deter many traders from venturing in it. Again, the higher the risk, the higher the returns and the vice versa holds, A standard account trader has a higher risk of loss because if a lot falls with 100 pips, he or she loses $1000. Such loses can be devastating for beginner traders.

Managed Trading Accounts

Managed accounts are accounts where one puts in the capital but does not make the decisions to sell or buy. Such accounts are handled by account managers such as stockbrokers and stock managers. In this case, the traders set objectives for the managers (the expected returns, risk management) and the managers have to meet them.

Managed accounts are categorized into two major types namely Pooled funds and Individual accounts. In pooled funds, the money of different investors is put into an investment vehicle referred to as mutual fund and the profits generated are shared. The accounts are further classified by risk tolerance. If a trader is looking for higher returns, he or she may put his money in a high risk/reward account while those looking for long term steady income can invest in lower risk accounts. Under managed accounts, the individual accounts are managed by a broker each in its own capacity, unlike the pooled funds where the manager uses all the money together.

The main advantage of managed accounts is that one gets professional advice and guidance. An experienced professional forex account manager will be making the decisions and this is a benefit that one can use. Again, a trader gets to trade without having to spend hours analyzing the charts and watching for developments.

One disadvantage that deters traders from venturing into this account is the high price. One should be aware that the majority of managed accounts require one to put in at least $2000 in the pooled account and $10000 for the individual accounts. To add to this cost, the managers are entitled to a commission which is calculated monthly or yearly. The managed accounts are also very inflexible for the trader. If he or she sees an opportunity to trade, he or she will not be able to make a move but will rely on the manager to decide.

Note

It is advisable for a swing trader to use the demo accounts offered by brokers before investing in real money regardless of the account he or she opts to use. Demo accounts allow one to practice without risk and also to try out different strategies. One rule that every trader should apply is to never invest in a real account unless they are completely satisfied with it. One of the main differences between success and failure in forex exchange is the account selected.

Opening an Account

Forex exchange has been around for very many years and some say that it is as old as the invention of national currencies. Over the years, the market has grown so much so that it is the biggest market across the world. However, it has not been accessible to the public as easily as it is today. From the 1990s when the era of the internet begun, many retail forex brokers have established routes through which anyone can trade in currencies so long as they can access the internet and have some money. There is a lot of hype and information about forex trade on the internet but not everybody understands how to select and open an account.

Currently, opening a forex account has become as easy as opening a bank account or another type of brokerage account. Some of the typical requirements are a name, phone number, address, email, a password, account currency type, country of citizenship, date of birth, employment status, and tax id or Social security number. Opening an account may also require one to answer some financial questions such as their net worth, annual income, trading objectives, and trading experience. Before one starts to trade on the foreign exchange market, they should make some considerations to ensure that they have a positive, secure and successful experience.

The Right Broker

The first step to trading well is to find the right broker. The activities of forex exchange are decentralized and there are hardly any regulations. Because of the over the counter nature, traders are advised to identify a reliable broker. This involves conducting researches on the reputation of the broker; to identify if there is a history of irregular practices. One may also want to comprehensively understand the services offered by the particular broker before setting up an account. While some brokerages support basic and plain vanilla activities, others offer very sophisticated trading platforms. Some brokers will offer the trader analytical resources to support better decision making while others won't.

Again, a trader should assess the fees and commissions for different brokers. Majority of Brokers charge some fees for their services through the bid-ask spread and in many cases, it is not a large percentage. However, some brokerages have some other fees and commissions and they might be hidden from the trader. When one is considering the extra costs, he or she should check if it is worthwhile.

The Procedure

Opening a foreign exchange account is not hard but traders should have a few things to get started. The trader will have to provide some identification information such as name, phone number, country of origin et cetera. Besides, the trader will be required to state his or her trade intentions and their level of knowledge and experience in the trade. The steps of opening an account may vary depending on the brokerage firm but normally it involves:

- Accessing the website of the broker and study the accounts available. The accounts include small ones where the trader can trade with minimum capital such as mini accounts or the sophisticated accounts designed for experienced traders such as standard trading account.

- Completing an application form,

- Getting registered (user name and password) to access the account.

- Log in to the client portal and arrange for a transfer of money from the bank to the forex account. These deposits can be done through credit or debit card, checks, or electronic transfers.

- Once the funds are transferred, the trader is ready to start trading. Before trading, the trader may review the recommendations made by the brokers or extra services offered such as simulator programs.

Online Trading

It refers to buying and selling stocks or other assets by the use of a broker's internet-based website or trading platform. Currencies, futures, options, ETFs, mutual funds, bonds, and stocks can all be traded online. It is called self-directed investing or e-trading. As mentioned above, in a split of a second you can trade stocks and other financial instruments such as the Dollar or Euro, some commodities such as Gold or Oil as well as main market indices.

One more advantage of online trading is that the improvement in the rate of which trades can be implemented and settled, since there is no demand for paper-based files to be reproduced, registered and entered into a digital format. Once an investor opens a buy position on the internet, the trade is set in a database that assesses for the very best price by searching all of the marketplace trades that trade the inventory in the investor's currency. The market with the very best price fits the buyer with a vendor and sends the confirmation to the purchaser's agent and the seller's agent. All this process can be achieved within minutes of opening a trade, in comparison to making a telephone call that requires several confirmation steps before the representative can input the purchase. It is all up to investors or stock traders to do their research about a broker before opening trading accounts with the business. Before an account is opened, the customer will be requested to complete a questionnaire about their investment and financial history to ascertain which sort of trading accounts is acceptable for the customer. On the flip side, an experienced trader who would love to execute various trading strategies will be provided with a margin account where he can purchase, brief, and compose securities such as shares, options, futures, and currencies. Not all securities are all readily available to be traded on the internet, depending upon your broker. Some agents need you to call them to put a transaction on any shares trading on the pink sheets and choose stocks trading over-the-counter. Additionally, not all agents ease derivatives trading in currencies and commodities throughout their affiliate platforms. Because of this, it is necessary that the dealer knows what a broker offers before registering with the trading platform.

Most online trading classes are centered on instructing marketplace mechanisms and technical evaluation, while others might concentrate on more specific strategies or particular asset classes. Courses may offer a comprehensive summary of technical analysis in addition to other strategies designed for specific asset classes. They assist traders quickly reach a stage where they are comfortable creating approaches and executing trades.

Fundamental analysis.

Of the two most broadly perceived swing trading styles, swing exchanging and utilizing a purchase to hold venture system, swing exchanging is by a long shot the most appropriate style for alternatives. The purchase to hold procedure is not generally reasonable by any means, since choices are essentially momentary exchanging instruments. Most contracts lapse following a couple of months or shorter, and even the more extended term leaps typically terminate following one year. Accordingly, alternatives are the ideal device for swing exchanging. Swing trading is much less exceptional than day exchanging and furthermore significantly less tedious. With day exchanging, you must be set up to spend the entire day checking the business sectors while trusting that the ideal time will enter and leave positions. The degrees of focus required can be extremely depleting, and it requires an unmistakable range of abilities to be fruitful utilizing this style. Swing exchanging, then again, is an ideal center ground for those that need to see a sensibly brisk profit for their cash yet do not have room schedule-wise to devote to purchasing and sell throughout the day, consistently.

It's an incredible style for those that are relative amateurs and those that hold down all day occupations or have other time responsibilities during the working day. It's conceivable to feature potential swings, enter the important position, and afterward simply check how your position is faring toward the finish of every day, or even every couple of days, before choosing whether or not to leave that position. The nuts and bolts of this style are generally simple to get to grasps with, which is another valid justification for giving it a go. You do not have a colossal measure of information to begin with; you simply need to know how choices work and be set up to devote a sensible measure of time to searching for the correct chances. There are definitely dangers included, however this style to a great extent empowers you to go out on a limb that you are alright with despite everything it allows you to make some better than average benefits. You can set stop misfortunes or use spreads so you are never in peril of losing more cash than you are alright with. You can really utilize spreads in an assortment of systems, some of which are especially valuable for swing exchanging when you are not for all time checking value changes in the market.

Guidance for Swing Trading Options

Arranging and investigating are significant for anybody hoping to utilize this style. You ought to be solid and steady and have a smart thought of precisely what sorts of examples and patterns you are searching for and what kind of exchanges you are going to make in some random circumstance. You do need there to be a sure measure of adaptability in the manner you exchange, yet it can have an unmistakable arrangement of targets and a characterized arrangement for how you will accomplish those objectives. The market can be eccentric so you should probably change in like manner. Anyway a strong arrangement in any event gives you a stage to work from.

It is a smart thought to set most extreme misfortunes on any position that you enter. It's improbable that you will get your expectations and conjectures right every time you enter a position, and some of the time the costs will move against you. You ought to dependably be set up to cut your misfortunes and escape a terrible position; it can and will occur and you simply need to ensure that your great exchanges exceed your awful exchanges. Great expository abilities are valuable. You don't need to settle on choices as fast as though you were day exchanging so you have room schedule-wise to investigate circumstances and work out the best passage and leave purposes of a specific example or pattern that you distinguish. It's likewise imperative to be persistent. In the event that you can't locate a decent section point to exploit a value swing, at that point you need the control and tolerance to hold up until an open door presents itself. You don't should make exchanges each day if there are no reasonable ones to be made, and the way to progress is extremely about picking the correct chances and executing your exchanges at the opportune time. Correspondingly, you ought to dependably have an objective benefit for a position, and close your position when you have made that benefit. Attempting to press additional benefit out of a vacant position can simply bring about losing your benefits. You can undoubtedly set your parameters for constraining misfortunes and securing benefits by utilizing stop orders, alternatives spreads, or a mix of the both.

Alternatives Brokers for Swing Trading Options

A standout amongst the most significant choices you have to make before beginning with this, or some other style, is which stock merchant would it be advisable for you to utilize? Utilizing an online intermediary is not as fundamental for swing exchanging for what it's worth for day exchanging, yet you could utilize a customary representative in the event that you needed. Be that as it may, there are as yet numerous points of interest to utilizing an online merchant; for instance they by and large offer less expensive charges and commissions which will enable you to put in your requests.

Financial Instruments For Swing

Whether you know it or not, you're already ahead of almost all the novice traders out there and most of the unsuccessful traders as well. The idea of taking the order flow into account when determining your strategy is not something you will read about too much so take the time to really study this well. It will be alien at first, especially if you've read other books which promise magical indicators, but you will reap the rewards of your effort.

When determining their strategy in the markets, most traders make the mistake of sticking to one method and try to fit it to multiple market environments (or landscapes). This is an absurd thing to do. Would you wear just swimming trunks when the weather outside is below zero? Would you bundle up in 4 layers when it's 100 degrees outside? Yet again, we see how common sense gets thrown out of the window for some reason when it comes to trading.

Everything comes down to (if you're following along, you know what's coming next) order flow.

Order Flow and Your Strategies

The order flow determines the charting landscape and the landscape determines your strategy. It really is that simple. It doesn't matter which indicator you use, which magical formula or mathematical regression tactic, it all comes down to which phase or what type of order flow is currently present.

This is what makes it possible to make money using a simple moving average strategy (we'll explain this later) as well as with a far more complicated indicator. Indicators which are meant to indicate trend direction and characteristics of a trend must be used in trending environments. Indicators which oscillate between extremes must be used in a ranging environment.

Easy to Understand, Tough to Follow

It's easy enough to say 'use this in a trend' and 'use this in a range'. Technically you can get away with just two indicators right? Well, right! However, the key point is identifying what is a trending environment and what is a range. You see, markets rarely move in a uniform fashion. You will see trends with big counter-trend participation, ranges which move in a channel and at a slight angle, etc. It's very rare to see a strong, explosive move which sustains itself over long period of time or to see a clean range with the upper and lower boundaries being cleanly respected. So what's the solution? Well, you can't change the market's behavior. Hence, you need to modulate and determine what your behavior is going to be, given the market environment. If you're unable to determine what's going on, as previously mentioned, simply step aside and wait. When you're a novice, the best things you can do for your own sake is to wait and watch. Unfortunately, most novices do the exact opposite and rush to trade. A good idea is to perhaps develop some sort of graded scale to help you determine the strength of the trend. The stronger the trend, the lesser the number of counter-trend traders. The weaker the trend, the greater the number of counter-trend traders.

A range would of course be the weakest possible trend present in the markets given that it has equally balanced order distribution.

You could decide to trade only the strongest trends and the most obvious ranges; in other words, both extremes of the graded scale you develop. Over time, as your skill grows, you expand to cover more scenarios and thus build your confidence. As mentioned before, there is no magic pill here you can take. The only way forward is via persistent hard work.

A Simple Execution Checklist

In lieu of the above, it would be best for you to develop an execution checklist. It could be as follows:

- Is price in a trend or range? Or can't say?

- How strong is the trend (if in a trend)? How defined/clean is the range (if in a range)? Assign a number on the scale if using one.

- Is this number something I'm comfortable with to participate further?

- If so, what are my trend strategies (if in a trend)? What are my range strategies (if in a range)?

- Execute.

Again, this is easy to write down but difficult to execute because of the highly charged trading environment newbies partake in. The mental aspect of trading is an important skill you must master if you are to succeed. For now, just remember what was said earlier about the ideal trading state being one of slightly bored attachment. If you are not in this state, then do not trade.

When to and When Not to

At this point, it would serve us well to list out a few do's and don'ts of trading.

Do not trade if:

- Your state is one of over excitement or action seeking.

- Your state is depressed, sad or overwhelmed.

- You feel hurried or rushed and feel like there's too much going on and can't keep up.

- You want to make money in a hurry and NOW!

- You think you've found the ultimate strategy which unlocks all market secrets.

- You're dreaming of luxury cars and mansions and total financial independence.

Do trade if:

- You recognize how much more you need to learn and are determined to put in the work.

- You know you are willing and ready to step aside and admit "I don't know."

- You are risking only what you can afford to lose as capital.

- You are realistic about your money goals. The world's biggest hedge funds consider a 15% annual return a brilliant performance. You're OK with producing this much amount of money from your trading.

This chapter has strayed a bit beyond the technical aspects of trading and into the mindset and risk portion of your trading skills. For now, you must understand that your trading success depends on much more than just your technical strategy. You need to master risk management as well as your mindset.

Ideally, you will start working on your mindset first, then your risk management and then finally on your technical strategy. With most people though, this is reversed. This is OK as long as you work on all aspects and not just the technical portion, expecting some secret to be unlocked via some unknown indicator. You might as well learn now that no such thing exists. Never has and never will.

Successful traders make money via mastery in all three aspects of trading: Technical Skills, Mindset and Risk Management. It behooves you to master all aspects of all three.

Now with that little warning, it is time to delve into the individual indicators and strategies you can use with them as part of your technical plan to trade. They're great tools but they need to be used appropriately. No one ever built a cabinet using a hammer to drive screws after all.

When it comes to trading on the stock market, financial instruments are the specific asset that you are trading each time you buy and sell new stocks. Financial instruments represent stocks, bonds, commodities, currencies, and any other valuable instrument that can be traded within a company. From the market perspective, there are five major financial instruments that you can trade: exchange-traded funds (ETFs), individual stocks, currencies, crypto-currencies, and options. We are going to discuss what each of these are in this chapter, and which you should consider trading as a beginner.

Even if you are only planning on becoming involved in one particular financial instrument, such as ETFs or options, it is important that you educate yourself on what the other forms of financial instruments are. This way, if and when you are ready to diversify your portfolio, you have a strong idea of what else you can get into trading and how it works. Furthermore, as you read through blogs and various news articles to keep up to date on the market, you are going to see these terms being used in plenty of scenarios. Knowing what you are reading about can help you educate yourself, further improving your ability to make educated decisions on your own trades.

Exchange-Traded Funds (ETFs)

Exchange-traded funds, or ETFs, are the most popular financial instrument to be traded amongst beginners. When you trade an ETF, rather than trading something specific such as an individual stock or a commodity, you are trading more of a financial basket which keeps several different financial instruments in it. Most ETFs are made up of individual stocks, commodities, bonds, or even a mixture of these particular financial instruments. The "basket" or ETF is then awarded an associated price that can easily be bought and sold. As the ETF is bought and sold, the price fluctuates, which means that ETF prices fluctuate more than virtually any other financial instrument on the market.

Some ETFs are US only, whereas others can be traded internationally. Before you get involved in buying and selling stocks with ETFs it is a good idea to do your research and get an idea of where yours can be bought and sold, as this will help you educate yourself on whether or not it is worth your investment. Regarding ETFs, their fees are often quite a bit lower than any other financial instrument that you can trade. The commissions paid to your brokerage are going to be significantly lower than they would be if you bought each stock individually, which means that you are actually going to end up with more money in your pocket at the end of the day, too. I strongly recommend that when you start out with swing trading you start out with ETFs, as they are going to be the easiest for you to understand. This way, too, rather than having to research and follow various different individual stocks, you can simply follow one ETF.

Although ETFs are simple and continue to be the best trades that you can make, it is important to understand that there are some drawbacks to trading in them. One of the biggest drawbacks is that people tend to become complacent and trade exclusively in one form of stock or another, and never fully diversify their portfolio. In certain ETFs this is not necessarily so bad because the fund itself is diversified, but if you trade in something more specific such as commodities, this can massively reduce your diversification. As well, if you do choose to have your ETFs actively managed by a brokerage, it can cost more, so it is truly best to learn how to do it yourself. Spending money on a brokerage will only cut into your earnings unnecessarily.

Individual Stocks

When people get started investing in the stock market, what they often expect they are going to be investing in are individual stocks. Investing in individual stocks is not ideal for beginners because they are harder to track and their patterns are more volatile and less predictable than other stocks. With individual stocks, you really need to be able to gauge the likely success or growth of a company to be able to predict whether or not the valuation of your stocks is going to improve enough over time to make the trade worth it.

Many times, when individual people get invested in individual stocks they are doing so to diversify their portfolio, as well as to take the gamble at earning more from their investments. That is because, as with anything, the higher risk of individual stocks can also lead to a higher reward from stocks.

If you do decide to get involved in individual stocks, you should be prepared to pay higher brokerage fees, or to have to engage in far more trades on your own. You should also be prepared to follow the market much more closely as you are going to need to know exactly what is going on in your particular stock, so that you can buy and sell at the right times. If you are not following the market closely, you could find yourself missing out on massive amounts of profits in a relatively short amount of time. As a result, you can completely destroy your ability to earn any significant income from this particular trade method. Beyond the additional fees and market research you are going to have to do, buying and selling individual stocks also requires a high amount of personal discipline as you are going to need to be able to avoid making emotional decisions in your trades. For many people, it can be challenging to hold on when the market drops greatly, as you may have an intense fear that it will never come back up for that particular stock. As a result, you could drastically short yourself on earnings due to emotional decisions, when in reality what you should have been doing was holding on and waiting for the market to balance out again. Unless you have a strong sense of personal discipline, a clear understanding of the market, experience with trading, and the willingness to invest more time and money into your trades, you should refrain from using individual stocks. These are better reserved for people who have already invested a healthy amount into other stocks, such as ETFs, and who are interested in playing around and taking larger risks with a smaller amount of their investable funds. This way, you are not at risk of losing everything due to a poor investment choice.

Trading Currencies

When it comes to trading currencies: it is exactly what you would expect. You buy currency and sell it. Trading currencies is actually largely what places a certain numerical value on each currency, and is directly responsible for the strengths and weaknesses in the values of different currencies. Typically, currencies that are commonly traded are worth far more, whereas those that are not traded nearly as often are not worth quite as much. When it comes to trading currencies, the market is open 24 hours a day from Monday morning to Friday evening. They close for the weekends, but are otherwise open nonstop. A person that trades currencies trades in what is known as "lots," which suggests the amount or lot of currency that you are trading. 1,000 is a lot of $1,000 in the base currency, and is known as a "micro lot." Mini lots are 10,000 or $10,000 or your base currency, and standard lots are 100,000 or $100,000 of your base currency. Unlike individual stocks, where you can buy and sell just one single stock, you trade currencies in what is known as pairs, meaning that you buy one currency and then sell another. If you choose to trade in currency, there are 18 commonly traded currencies that can be paired together to create your trades. While many other currencies exist, they are not traded on the market, which means that you cannot buy and sell them. Of the 18 currencies that you can buy and trade on the market, only 8 of them are incredibly popular to trade. Those 8 currencies include: the Canadian Dollar (CAD), the U.S. Dollar (USD), the British Pound (GBP), the Euro (EUR), the New Zealand Dollar (NZD), the Swiss Franc (CHF), the Japanese Yen (JPY), and the

Australian Dollar (AUD). Although you can certainly trade with the other 10, most trades happen exclusively in these currencies, and you should stick with them too if you are going to get into currency trading.

Risk And Account Management

Risk management is a deliberate action taken by a trader or investor. The purpose is to keep losses at a minimum. As a trader, you are exposed to a lot of dangers. You can lose money if you are not careful or if your strategy was not successful. Should you lose money in a trade, then the risk can be managed. All that you need to do is to open yourself up to being profitable in the market.

Risk management is a grossly neglected area of every unsuccessful trader's strategy. Indeed, most do not even understand the concept and fail to explore it beyond the cursory nod given to stop losses and per trade risk.

Perfect risk management can save a poor strategy but even the best strategy cannot save poor risk management. Many of you must have heard of this piece of wisdom but probably very few of you truly understand its implications.

Risk in trading is quite simple. It is the probability of you losing your capital on a series of trades, including the current one.

Plan Your Trades

Some of the best tools you will need as part of your risk management plan are take-profit and stop-loss. Using these two tools, you can plan your trades in advance. You will need to use technical analysis in order to determine these two points. With this information, you should be able to determine the price you are willing to pay as well as the losses you can incur.

Adhere to a Proven Trading Method

Furthermore, do not transform it. In the event that you have a demonstrated technique however it does not appear to work in a given exchanging session, do not return home that night and attempt to devise another. In the event that your strategy works for more than one-portion of the exchanging sessions, at that point stay with it. Keep in mind, the Holy Grail of exchanging is cashing the executives.

Consistency is Confidence

How great does it feel have the option to turn on your exchanging stage the morning realizing that, on the off chance that you play by the guidelines, the likelihood of fruitful exchanging day is generally high? The appropriate response? Great! Keep in mind: If you make somewhat consistently, at that point you have earned the privilege to exchange greater.

Try not to Chase the Markets

Proficient merchants that pick Admiral Markets will be satisfied to realize that they can exchange totally chance free with a FREE demo exchanging account. Rather than going to the live markets and putting your capital in danger, you can dodge the hazard out and out and essentially practice until you are prepared to change to live exchanging.

Pursue Your Trading Routine

Never attempt to break your exchanging schedule. Pursue real markets and exchange just during the significant markets. These include: New York, London and Tokyo markets. The value moves all the more detectably during significant market sessions, so you can disregard minor markets. Significant markets furnish you with an incredible number of arrangements as well.

Maintaining a trading Journal

You can do this online or keep a paper copy nearby. When you are done with one trade, make sure to write down what happened during that trade, what strategy you used, what was going on in the market, how much you spent, and more. If you ever get stuck with one of your trades or you aren't sure how to handle one situation or another, you can refer back to this journal and see what advice it has. You may be surprised that, after a particularly hard situation in a different trade, you can look back in this journal and find the answers that you need. More than anything else, your trade journal is what will keep your risk management on track. Your journal should, at a minimum, record your trade date, instrument, direction (long or short), stop loss size, reasons for entering, exit date, P/L and any comments. As a trader, you need to keep a journal so that you have a reliable record of your trades and their performance. This is one of the best ways of learning about your style and performance. Trade tracking journals also enables you to track your trades and the actions you took during certain situations and instances.

In short, a trading journal provides traders with the necessary tools and information that they need to evaluate their trading activities objectively.

As a trader, you really should be tracking your trades throughout the day. A journal helps you to keep a record of the happenings each day as well as your reactions or actions. Your plan should include a tried and tested system that suits your trading style. Make sure that you test this system and review it often then improve your trading plans and performance.

Setting Target and Stops

We can define a stop-loss as the total amount of loss that a trader is willing to incur in a single trade. Beyond the stop-loss point, the trader exits the trade. This is basically meant to prevent further losses by thinking the trade will eventually get some momentum. We also have what is known as a take-profit point. It is at this point that you will collect any profits made and possibly exit a trade. At this point, a particular stock or other security is often very close to the point of resistance. Beyond this point, a reversal in price is likely to take place. Rather than lose money, you should exit the trade. Traders sometimes take profit and let a particular trade continue if it was still making money. Another take-profit point is then plotted. If you have a good run, you are allowed to lock in the profits and let the good run continue.

Assessing Risk versus Reward

A lot of traders tend to think of the outcome of their trade in terms of the amount they make, that is, $100 or -$50 and so on. This is a warped way of thinking since it places an undue amount of importance on the amount of money one makes. This is not to say it's unimportant but the best way to make money trading isn't in following this method. Instead, you need to measure the outcome of your trades as a function of your risk per trade, that is, as a multiple of your R (R being the percent of your capital you risk per trade). Thus on a loss, your profit/loss record (P/L) will read -R and on a win your P/L will read 1.5R or 2R and so on. Recording it this way puts the focus squarely on your risk management and forces you to think in terms of risk. A lot of traders lose a lot of money at the markets for a very simple reason. They do not know about risk management or how to go about it. This mostly happens to beginners or novice traders. Most of them simply learn how to trade then rush to the markets in the hope of making a kill. Sadly, this is now how things work because account and risk management are not taken into consideration. Think about it this way. Supposing someone you don't trust many approaches you for a $1,000 loan with a promise to pay you back with $100 interest after a month. You may be hesitant because the risk is greater compared than the profit. However, if he promises to pay you back after one month with a $2,000 interest, then the risk is well worth it. The ratio of risk versus reward, in this case, is 2:1. A lot of investors believe this to be an excellent ratio and many would take it because they get a chance to double their money.

If the borrower offered to pay back $3,000, then the risk vs. reward ratio increases to 3:1.

A trader who is unsuccessful will likely look at an entry and then only think about the profit they will make on that trade. But, a trader who is successful is always going to consider the upside and the downside with any trade they choose. So, they are going to think about how much of a risk they are going to have if they take a loss. It is all about comparing the amount of risk that you are going to take to the reward that you are hoping to get from that trade.

For the reward, they are hoping that the XBI stock is going to reach $91.00 for each share or the prior area of resistance. This can help them earn $3.50 a share for this one. This means that, in this scenario, the risk is $1.00 a share, but the reward is a potential $3.50 a share. This ends up being a very good risk to reward ratio. If the reward only ended up being $0.75 a share, then it is best to look for another option since the risk is too high for that trade.

Always ensure to apply the risk versus reward ratio for all your trades. Keep in mind the indicated acceptable levels. If you are unable to find acceptable ratios after trying several times, find another security. Once you learn how to incorporate risk management into your trades, you will become safer as you trade without incurring any huge losses.

Managing the Trade Size

As a trader, you also need to make determinations regarding other aspects of the trade. These include the number of stock or currency or any other financial markets' instruments. When doing this, most traders overlook position size. They feel like it is not important enough or sometimes they have no clue that it is necessary and how to determine an optimum one.

Some traders have large accounts and wish they could spend freely. These usually employ different approaches when it comes to position size. Even if you had an account worth $500,000, then you would not want to risk over $500 per trade. This is equivalent to 1% of the total amount in the account.

Sometimes, people choose stop levels for the day. These are daily stop orders issued by a client to their broker and so on. Daily stop-loss points simply indicate the amount of money that you are ready to lose per trade. Should this level be attained as you trade, then you will have to stop trading and exit all other possible positions in the market.

Experienced traders usually opt to equate the daily stop-loss positions as equivalent to their average profitability. So if a person makes $400, then their stop loss order will be a lot closer to this figure.

Keep Your Emotions in Check

Keeping your emotions in check is especially important when you find a stock going against you. Not only does this make you realize that you made a mistake during your analysis and any calculations, which carries its own emotions, but this can also make you go through a series of emotional stages. There are many traders and investors who state that this series of five stages is similar to the five stages of grief.

Follow the 1% Rule

One of the biggest ways to reduce your risk is to make sure that you focus on keeping your proportion low. One of the best ways to do this is to only risk about 1% of the money in your account with each trade. For example, if you have $10,000 in your account, this means that you will not trade more than $100 on a trade. However, many expert swing traders believe that when you are first starting out, you should lower this even more. Therefore, a beginner should look at trading no more than around 0.3% to 0.5%. While this doesn't seem like a lot of money, most stocks generally aren't a large amount of money to buy. Some of the most expensive stocks to buy will be blue-chip stocks.

Determine a Stop-Loss Amount

After you have looked at setting your risk at 1%, you can look at another factor, which is setting your trade risk. This is when you set your stop-loss amount. This amount will be created when you set up your trading plan. For example, if you spent $10.00 on your trade, then you might set up your stop-loss level at $9.80.

This means that once you reach this amount, you will sell that stock and only lose .20 cents. Most traders will look at the percentage of their account they put towards their stock in order to help them determine their stop-loss amount. This is because some traders might feel more comfortable setting their stop-loss amount at a higher percentage if they followed the 1% rule than an if they decided to go up to 3% or even 5%.

Follow Your Guidelines and Rules

As you get started in your trading career, you will start to develop your own rules and guidelines, such as in your trading plan. It is important that you don't change any of these rules and guidelines without fully looking at your trade as a whole. On top of this, it is important to follow because it will help keep you focused, you will begin to learn the details of swing trading easier as you won't be so concerned about your next step, and you will feel more comfortable in your abilities.

Fundamental Analysis

Fundamental analysis can be described as a method of evaluating securities such as stocks. The aim is to measure the intrinsic value of a company or its stock. We carry out fundamental analysis by closely examining financial reports, economic prospects, as well as other quantitative and qualitative factors. Basically, you study anything that pertains to the value of the company's security.

There are plenty of professionals who conduct stock and company analysis. They include traders such as stock traders, stock analysts, fund managers, and many others. As a swing trader, you need to learn how to carry out a thorough fundamental analysis of any stock or security that you are interested in. Fundamental analysis is the backbone of any investment process. You can only be regarded as a successful trader or investor if you can successfully perform fundamental analysis.

When we talk of fundamentals, we actually mean the quantitative and qualitative data that significantly contributes to the success and financial valuation of a company. It also includes an assessment of both macroeconomics and microeconomics aspects. These are aspects that are essential for determining the worth of a company or other assets.

Microeconomics and Macroeconomics

Macroeconomics stands for all factors that affect the general economy. These are factors such as inflation, supply and demand, unemployment and even GDP growth. They also include international trade and prevailing monetary and fiscal policies put forth by the authorities. Macroeconomic considerations are useful when it comes to matters of large-scale analysis of the economy and how these relate to business activities.

Microeconomic factors are those that focus on the smaller elements of the economy. These include elements in certain particular sectors of a market. For example, labor issues in a given market, matters such as supply and demand and others such as labor and consumer issues relating to the said industry.

An Example One of the world's most successful stock analysts and traders is Warren Buffet. He uses fundamental analysis to determine which shares to buy and which companies to invest in. His success as an analyst has turned him into a billionaire. Apart from analyzing companies, the equities market can also be analyzed. There are some analysts who conducted a fundamental analysis of the S&P 500 for a period of a week. This was from 4th July to 8th July 2016. Within this period of time, the S&P index went up to 2129.90 following the release of an impressive jobs report within the US. This was an unprecedented performance surpassed only by the May 2015 which was 2132.80. The superb performance was attributed to the announcement of 287,000 new jobs across the country.

Intrigues of Fundamental Analysis

Some of the parameters that analysts look at within a company's financial statement include a measure of solvency, profitability, liquidity, growth trajectory, efficiency, and leverage. Analysts also use rations to work out the financial health of companies. Examples of such ratios include quick ratio and current ratio. These rations are useful in determining a company's ability to repay short-term liabilities based on their current assets.

To find the current ratio, you will divide the current assets with the current liabilities. These figures can easily be accessed from the company's balance sheet. While there is no ratio that is considered ideal, anything below 1 is considered a poor financial situation that is incapable of meeting all short-term debts.

The balance sheet also provides analysts with additional information such as current debt amounts owed by the company. In such a situation, then the analysis will focus on the debt ratio. This is computed by working out all the liabilities and dividing by the total assets. When the ratio is computed, a ratio greater than 1 points to a company with a lot more debt compared to its assets. This means that should interest rates rise, then the firm may default on its debts.

Stock Analysis

Stock analysis can be defined as the process used by traders and investors to acquire in-depth information about stock or company. The analysis is done by evaluating and studying current and past data about the stock or even company. This way, traders and investors are able to gain a significant edge in the market as they will be in a position to make well-informed decisions.

The stock analysis involves not just current financial reports but also compares the current financial statements with those from previous years. This will give a trader or investor a feel of the company's performance and will determine whether the firm is stable, receding, or growing. It is also common for an analyst to compare a company's financial statement with those of other companies in the same sector. This is done in order to compare profitability and other parameters.

Of great importance is the operating profit. It is a measure of the revenue that a company is left with after other expenses have been cleared. Basically, a firm with operating margins of 0.27 is viewed favorably when compared with one whose margin is 0.027, for instance. This can be translated to mean that the firm whose operating margin is 0.27 spends 73 cents per dollar earned to foot its operating costs.

Benefits of Undertaking Fundamental Analysis

There are lots of benefits of conducting a thorough fundamental analysis of a company. Here is a look at some of these benefits.

1. Long-term Trends

Fundamental analysis is excellent for investors and traders, especially long-term investors. Patient investors looking to invest in the long term as well as traders seeking solid, reliable companies will definitely benefit from the analysis.

2. Identification of Valuable Companies

The reliable fundamental analysis enables investors and traders to identify firms that are of high value and worth investing in. A lot of notable investors always look for valuable companies. They include John Neff and Warren Buffet. Valuable companies will have a strong balance sheet, staying power, stable earnings, and valuable assets.

3. Business Acumen

Fundamental analysis will help you develop a deep understanding of the business. For instance, you will become familiar with profit drivers and revenue sources of the company. For instance, earning expectations and actual earnings are extremely useful when it comes to equity and stock prices.

Technical Analysis

This is another method used by analysts, investors, and traders to analyze stocks and companies. This type of analysis pays closer attention to previous market action and how this can be used to predict future performance. In this instance, an analyst, or trader, will analyze the entire market and will focus their attention on volume and price. Other factors looked at include supply and demand as well as any essential factors that can move the market.

One of the most crucial tools for technical analysis is a chart. Charts are key for successful analysis of any market or particular stocks or companies. They provide a graphical presentation of stock and its trend within a given time period. For instance, a technical analyst can use a chart to indicate some areas as either resistance or support levels.

Resistance levels are placed above a stock's prevailing market price while support levels are indicated by previous lows that occur just below the current or prevailing market price. Should there be a break below support levels is a pointer to a bearish trend in the market. On the other hand, any break that occurs just above resistance levels will point to a bullish outlook.

Factors that Direct Technical Analysis

Technical analysis outcomes are only effective if the analysis of the price trend is affected by demand and supply forces. However, when other external factors come into play and affect price movement, then technical analysis of the stock may not be successful. For instance, stock prices can be affected by factors such as dividend announcements, the exit or death of company CEO, mergers, stock splits, change of management, monetary policy, and so on. It is common for analysts to conduct both technical and fundamental analysis together even though they can be conducted separately. Some choose to apply only one while others prefer both methods for stock and company analysis.

In order to come up with a successful investment strategy for your portfolio, then you will need to do some analysis and vet market sectors, stocks, and the markets.

Technical analysis is simply the process of forecasting the future movement of stocks on the markets according to past stock price movements. Just like weather predictions, technical analysis does not produce 100% accurate results.

However, technical analysis provides traders, and investors, with information which they can use to anticipate the price movement over time. There is a wide variety of charts that are used to help determine the future price movements of a particular stock.

Details of Technical Analysis

Technical analysis can be applied to numerous securities including Forex, stocks, futures, commodities, indices, and many more. The price of a security depends on a collection of metrics. These are volume, low, open, high, close, open interest, and so on. These are also known as market action or price data.

There are a couple of assumptions that we make as traders when performing technical analysis. However, remember that it is applicable only in situations where the price is only a factor of demand and supply. If there are other factors that can influence prices significantly, then the technical analysis will not work. The following assumptions are often made about securities that are being analyzed.

There are no Artificial Price Movements:

Artificial price movements are usually as a result of distributions, dividends, and splits. Such changes in stock price can greatly alter the price chart and this tends to cause technical analysis to be very difficult to implement. Fortunately, it is possible to remedy this. All that you need to do as an analyst is to make adjustments to historic data before the price changes.

The Stock is Highly Liquid:

Another major assumption that technical analysis makes is that the stock is highly liquid. Liquidity is absolutely crucial for volumes. When stocks are heavily traded as a result of liquidity and volume, then traders are able to easily enter and exit trades. Stocks that are not highly traded tend to be rather difficult to trade because there are very few sellers and buyers at any point in time. Also, stocks with low liquidity are usually poorly priced, sometimes at less than a penny for each share. This is risky as they can be manipulated by investors.

Study the Charts

Experts always advise traders to closely examine the chart of the stock they intend to buy as part of the technical analysis. When you examine the charts, you will be looking to spot the bottom and identify the best entry points. You will also examine the ceiling in order to identify the ideal exit points. All investors purchase stocks hoping the price will almost immediately go up. It is, therefore, crucial to look at and understand historic chart patterns of the particular stock.

The buy point can be looked at as the ground floor of a building where an elevator is about to rise to new highs. You do not only buy the right stock at the right price but also at the right time.

Cup with Handle Pattern

One of the most powerful patterns that allow consistency with stock purchase is the cup with handle pattern. This is the point where you buy a stock at its lowest price and is likely to rise very fast. Human nature is still the same where traders and other players in the markets exhibit either greed or fear.

What is Buy Point?

This is defined as the price level where stock is very likely to rise significantly. The buy point, also known as an entry point, is a point in the chart that offers the least resistance to a price increase.

Software for Technical Analysis

A key part of your life as a trader will involve the use of charts. In fact, there are those who believe that swing trader is only as productive as their charting software. You will spend a good amount of time reading charts and interpreting data on screens. Electronic trading platforms and market software are crucial resources of any serious trader. You can get most of the trading software from your preferred broker. There are other types of software programs available from software vendors. The trading software comes with a wide variety of functions including analysis functions, stock screening, research, and even trade.

In fact, trading software comes with in-built integrated additions like technical indicators, alert features, news, trade automation, fundamental analysis numbers, and much more.

Technical Analysis Charting Basics

Technical analysis is a method that answers the question of when to take or liquidate positions in markets or financial securities. It does so by analyzing historical prices and trading volumes via price chart patterns and technical measures or indicators.

Technical analysis is grounded on key assumptions:

• All possible information that can be gathered about a financial security or market, including financial and economic information, are already reflected on market prices, hence the focus on price;

• Trading volume is a strong indicator of market interest or disinterest in financial securities;

• Prices aren't as random as many think they are because it tends to follow general trends; and

• Because prices follow patterns that tend to repeat themselves over time, traders can learn to anticipate price movements of financial securities with fairly high accuracy.

Double Bottoms and Double Tops

The difference between the 2 is that the double bottom refers to a stock or market that is in a downtrend and potentially signaling a reversal to the upside. A double top is an upward trending stock that is signaling the potential to turn and start a downtrend in price.

The double bottom pattern resembles the shape of a "W" when looked at in a chart. A stock in a downtrend reaches an initial bottom, bounces higher for a short period of time, and then retests the low it made on the initial bottom. There is some market psychology involved with this "W" pattern. Once the initial bottom is put in and the stock moves higher, the buyers of the stock at much higher prices may see the bounce as an opportunity to cut their losses and get out at this higher price (fearing the stock is going to continue lower). Others who bought in on the first bottom may be short-term holders who are happy to take their small gain on the bounce. As the stock price drops back after the initial bounce higher, the value investors may be looking to get a second chance at buying the stock at this lower price. These buyers wait and then buy in at the initial support level created by the first bottom. The stock then starts to move higher again and forms the familiar "W" pattern. Traders who have been short the stock may add to the buying pressure once they see a strong level of support has been established. This pattern also works in reverse. The double top forms an "M" pattern instead of a "W" in the chart. The initial push higher and subsequent pullback is seen by some investors as an opportunity to take an entry or add to their existing position. Unfortunately for these new longs, the first top acts as a level of resistance and the second attempt to move higher fails. Some traders who are long the stock will see this failure to break higher and start to sell. Other traders who short stocks might also start selling because they see that an area of resistance has developed. The added short selling will create additional downward pressure on the stock price. The stock then continues lower on a reversal in price action.

Establishing the stop price on your potential trade is the key to managing your account and the risk that you take in a trade. Once a double bottom pattern is traced out, the low on the "W" pattern becomes the stop-loss price. Prior levels of resistance can be established as exit points, thus making it possible to calculate a risk to reward ratio.

If you can catch an entry near the second bottom on a long trade, then the difference between your entry price and that bottom price on the "W" should be relatively low. That low price difference creates a situation where you do not require a lot of upside in the price to get that 2 times reward you need in order to make this a good trade. Getting a good entry on a stock can make a big difference in your risk to reward ratio. The opposite applies to taking a short trade on a double top. Try to get an entry as near as possible to the second top which should give you the most desirable risk to reward ratio. Your stop will be around the high price of the topping pattern. If the price does start to continue higher, you should cover your short promptly to limit your losses.

How to trade Flag Pattern?

The bull flag starts with a strong price spike higher that often catches traders who are short the stock off-guard. The many market scanners do their work and identify the long opportunity, so momentum traders then get in long to help feed the buying frenzy and push the price higher. The breakout happens when the upper resistance line is broken as the price surges higher again.

As the stock's price breaks through the high of the formation, it triggers yet another breakout and uptrend move. The sharper the spike higher on the flagpole, the more powerful the bull flag move can be.

Bull flag

The opposite of the bull flag is referred to as the bear flag. It has the same chart pattern as the bull flag except it is inverted and results in the continuation of downward price action in a stock. The upside down flagpole starts with an almost vertical price drop due to the sellers being firmly in control of the price action. Downward moves in price can be much more aggressive than upward price action. However, nothing drops forever and at some point the traders who shorted the stock look to cover their positions and the value investors see a potential opportunity.

Bear flag

Similar to the bull flag, if the support and resistance lines are closer to horizontal, then the 2 entry points will be closer as well.

Flag patterns require a little patience while you wait for the flag to form after the initial run up or drop. Once you have recognized the beginning of the pattern, you should start to plot the upper and lower trend-lines as they form. These trend-lines will be one of your potential entry points and/or stop out levels.

You will usually have 2 possible entry spots on any flag formation in order to play the continuation of the trend.

The first entry will get you into the position a little earlier, which will allow you to profit more on the next surge in price action (up or down). The downside of getting in earlier is that there is always the potential for the stock to have a failed breakout and not move in the direction you expect. Waiting a little longer for the break in the top of the flag results in a little higher probability of a successful trade.

These flag patterns also give you 2 stop-loss price level options to use in case the stock does not move in the direction expected. If the stock fails to follow through and continue the trend, then the trendlines can provide a price level for a stop. On a downtrend, you would use the upper resistance line in the flag and in an uptrend you would use the lower support line.

The second stop-loss option is to use the low of the lowest candle in the bull flag and the high of the highest candle in a bear flag.

If you are a more conservative trader, you would use the closer stop price to keep losses to a minimum. However, this may result in getting stopped out of a trade that is becoming more volatile as the trend starts to continue. This means that, while you may take a smaller loss with this stop out price level, using this level may result in missing the move you were intending to play by getting stopped out due to some volatility in price. This volatility component is why some traders will give the trade a little more room to avoid having their stop triggered due to some volatility as opposed to a real direction change. Therefore, they will place their stop at the lower support trendline on uptrends and at the higher resistance trendline on downtrends.

A more sophisticated or experienced trader might use multiple entries and exits to offset some of the risks of entering the trade too early. A smaller percentage of the total trade in shares can be used as a starter position and then added to at the second point above or below the flagpole.

After the reversal, there are several bear flags formed on the overall trend down as bargain hunters think the bottom is forming and they go long. Traders who went short at the double top start taking profits, giving a temporary lift in the stock's price before the selling continues.

Before you enter a flag pattern, as an effective swing trader you should also be planning your targeted exit price or prices. You should be expecting at least 2 times the reward for the given risk that you're taking in the event that you get stopped out. You should look at prior longer-term levels of resistance as possible exit points if you go long and areas of support to exit if you go short. If you chose to enter at the break of the trend line, then your initial target can be set at the high or low of the flagpole. However, if the flag was close to horizontal, then that may not give you enough reward for the risk you are taking. You will have to look for other good exit points to get that 2 times reward you need to justify your trade. Other factors you may want to consider are the strength of the trend, overall market trends and the possible strength of the fundamentals driving the move. You may also consider scaling out of the position, which means taking some initial profits at the top of the flagpole by selling some of your position and then letting the remainder ride to your next expected level of resistance or support.

In this case, you must never let a winner turn into a loser. Lock in your profits and set your stop on the remainder at or near the entry price.

Bear and Bull Pendants

The bear and bull pendants are similar to the bear and bull flags described above. They start with a strong price move either up or down and then pause for a period of consolidation. The difference between the pendant and the flag is in the shape that the price action creates during this period of consolidation.

With a pendant, the range of price action narrows over the passage of time. When support and resistance lines are drawn off of the highs and lows, they come together in a point. The buyers and the sellers have been fighting it out and when the price action narrows to this point, often a winner finally emerges.

Usually the trend will continue after this narrowing period of consolidation, however, you should wait for a signal before taking an entry. Do not assume that the trend will continue and take an early entry. While you wait for the pattern to play out, take time to look at the daily charts and identify areas of support and resistance that have occurred in the past. Find potential profit target prices so you are prepared to do your risk to reward calculation in case you eventually consider an entry.

The narrowing price action is often compared to a coiled spring getting ready to pop one way or another.

You can find this narrowing price action on stocks that have been consolidating for days or weeks. These are also good stocks to watch because eventually either the buyers or sellers emerge in control and the ensuing price action can be strong.

ABCD Patterns

The ABCD pattern is another one of the basic and relatively easy patterns to recognize and trade. It is essentially a price move higher or lower, followed by a flag and then a continuation of a trend. As with much technical analysis-based trading, it often works because so many traders and computers are watching for the pattern and subsequently trading this setup.

This pattern is based on the principle that stock prices move in waves. These waves are due to the fact that price control is continually moving between the buyers and the sellers. If you examine a daily price chart of any stock, you will see waves of fluctuation up and down. Then, if you compare that daily chart to a weekly chart of the same stock, you will also see waves, but they will likely have larger price ranges because you're looking at a longer period of time. Within each one of those weekly bars there are 5 1-day bars, creating smaller waves inside bigger waves.

Knowing that stocks are moving in waves allows you to play on those waves much like a surfer. As a swing trader, you are waiting to catch and ride a wave, but like surfing, timing is very important. You will never see a surfer starting to paddle like crazy at the top of a wave to catch a ride.

They wait to begin their ride as the wave is just starting to approach. Similarly, a trader needs to anticipate the next wave and get on board at the beginning of the next move in price action.

Bullish ABCD patterns start with a strong upward move. The buyers are aggressively buying a stock from point A and consistently making new highs of the day (point B). You should not enter the trade here because at point B the price action is very extended. More importantly, your stop-loss will be way below your entry, giving you an extremely poor risk to reward ratio.

At point B, the traders who bought the stock earlier start selling it for profit and the price comes down. You should still not enter the trade because you do not know where the bottom of this pullback will be. However, if you see that the price does not come down from a certain level, such as point C, it means that the stock has found a potential support.

Bearish ABCD patterns are the reverse of the bullish pattern, with the stock price heading lower initially, and then there will be a bounce, which will be followed by a continuation lower.

The price action on this stock creates a very tradable pattern for a short trade. AMD pulls back from a high at point A to level B. It then forms a nice bear flag and also creates a double top when it fails to break through the previous high.

The stop-out price level on the short would be a break higher at about the $12.50 level. A failure of the stock to move higher would have allowed you to hold the position as it moved lower, possibly scaling out instead of selling the position for a profit all at once. By scaling out, you can lock in some profits and keep moving the stop out price lower as the price moves lower to maximize the gain on the trade.

How to Trade ABCD Patterns

The real key to trading this pattern is to watch for the pullbacks that inevitably occur when a stock makes a push higher or lower.

These patterns will often end with a double top or double bottom pattern. A topping pattern will usually have one or more gravestone type doji and the price action will struggle to make a new high and then ultimately fail and move lower. A bottoming pattern will be the reverse – one or more doji will make a dragonfly pattern signaling that the sellers are exhausted and the buyers are starting to take control. These signals do not necessarily have to appear but they help to confirm a setup for an entry on a trade.

Head and Shoulders Patterns

The head and shoulders chart pattern can be a top reversal signal and the so-called "inverted" head and shoulders pattern can be a bottom reversal pattern. This pattern is generally thought to be one of the most reliable swing trading patterns and therefore should be on your radar for stocks tracing out this type of price action.

The general pattern for the topping head and shoulders starts with a general uptrend in price action, which hits a peak and then slightly falls back or chops sideways for a period of time.

The stock then pushes higher through the previous peak and makes a new high before failing once again. Selling price action takes the stock back to the previous low after the first peak and the price action stays flat or bounces a little.

This price action in a chart traces the outline of a head and 2 shoulders; thus the name. A horizontal trend-line can be drawn across the 2 lows on the pullbacks and is referred to as the neckline. Once the price of the stock drops below this neckline, an established downtrend is in place and shorting the stock is now a tradable option.

Swing-Trading Rules

Simple Rules of Swing Trading

Rules are always there to help you be disciplined in what you are doing. Have you ever come across the swing trading rules before starting on trading? This chapter is all about covering the different rules of swing trading. The rules will guide you on the best ways on how to yield huge profits and incur minimum losses from swing trading. Below are some of the rules that will help you in your swing trading.

Simple Rules of Swing Trading

✔   **Select Volatile Markets.**

There are different markets in swing trading. To be successful in swing trading and be able to earn huge profits, you ought to choose a market with wider price fluctuations as compared to the narrower ones.

✔   **Consider Consistency.**

Consistency is the key to swing trading. You need to have a swing trading routine and always stick to it. Be consistent in what you are doing to prevent confusion and messing everything up. You ought to do much practice on the swing trading market to be familiar with all tips and tricks to be implemented. Practice this with the mock accounts you are provided with by the different brokers.

Mock accounts perfect your skills by providing virtual money to trade with. Be consistent with this practice before entering the real swing trading. Real trading in the swing market is all full of risks so you need to be fully prepared before making up your mind to start off.

✔ **Be Aware of Market Situations.**

A swing trading market has different situations. The market can either be bullish or bearish. You need to be aware of the market you are dealing with. Bearish markets are normally weak as compared to bullish markets. Be aware of the situation you are in the market so that you are able to make proper estimates of your profits and losses.

✔ **Do Not Take Chances.**

Do not be in the rush of making good money within a short period. Good things take time. Do not associate yourself in swing trading with gambling. You will lose a lot. Have patience with the money you are receiving, and with time, the money will of course increase. Do not utilize the chances since they will make you lose all the money that you worked hard for.

✔ **Accumulate Profits.**

Making a profit is always the main objective of any kind of business. You need to have a way of handling your profits made in swing trading. Profits need to be accumulated using different market strategies to prevent losses. The different market strategies may include implementing stop-loss orders on the stock when it reaches its resistance levels.

✔   **Be Aware of the Support and Level of Resistance.**

Support and the level of resistance are very crucial in swing trading. The stock in the swing trading market needs to be monitored. You need to be aware of its support and the level of resistance. The level of support and resistance on the stock are the prices on the trading chart at which a trader is able to tell if you have more buyers than sellers. The two factors aid to control the number of losses in the market.

✔   **Set Your Entry and Exit Points.**

Having an entry and exit plans in swing trading are very crucial. Sometimes the market behavior may not be as favorable as you accepted. Things and activities may go in vain. You need to have a plan to escape from this when it happens. Exit and entry point now come in handy. You are able to know how to work things out when the market is in its worst-case scenario. Always ensure to enter into the swing trading market with entry or exit plans to shun from making huge losses.

✔   **Take Advantage of the Stop-Loss Strategy.**

This is the kind of swing trading strategy that makes you be able to exit your position in the market. Stop-loss order when buying the stock is normally implemented at a position which allows a little change in the price fluctuations but becomes unfavorable when the market gets out of control.

Most swing traders purchasing stock use stop-loss when the price of the stock drops on the market.

Contrarily, when selling stock in the swing trading market, a stop-loss order can be implemented when there is a rise in the price of the stock since this is the resistance level of the underlying stock.

✔ **Minimize Losses.**

Losses are normally part of the game, but you need to do something when they become out of control. Losses affect your profits and your trading capital. You need to have some various working strategies on how to get rid of the losses in swing trading. Always implement the strategies when trading to succeed. If things are not working out well as expected, you need to quit what you are doing and work on something else.

Losses can make you lose a lot of money if you are not cautious while trading. The objectives of swing trading are all about raising profits and making investments and not making losses.

✔ **Have Control of Your Emotions.**

Do you know that emotions have made many traders fail in their trading? Emotions should not be part of any trader in the swing trading. Swing trading markets have both best-case and worst-case scenarios. You need to control your emotions when both scenarios happen in the market. You do not need to get over-excited when the market goes according to your favor. You need to be always alert not to drop tremendously.

Also, during your worst-case scenarios, do not get carried away with your emotions. Be strong and stop with the crying.

When things do not work out as you expected, find alternative actions immediately to be implemented in the market to avoid huge losses and risks in the swing trading market.

Do not feel bad when the mistakes happen in your trading, they are normally part of being successful in swing trading. Learn from the previous mistakes made to avoid repeating the mistakes next time you are trading. Mistakes normally make you grow and you learn a lot.

✔ **Have a Trading Plan.**

Who starts off something without a plan? You need to have a plan for everything. Swing trading requires a plan too. A trading plan guides you in all your activities. You are able to know the actions to be implemented in different market situations. A trading plan provides you with the desired market strategies and also assist in raising a reasonable amount of capital. A trading plan provides a routine for you and helps you become disciplined when you are trading.

A trading plan creates a schedule for your trading, in terms of the time and the type of trading you are dealing with. Also, a plan also enables you to come up with the goals and objectives of your trading. Objectives help you put much effort so as to achieve the goals. Do not enter into the swing trading market without a plan, it is a crucial factor that needs to be integrated with your trading.

✔ **Enjoy Swing Trading.**

Why does something you do not enjoy? Swing trading requires much passion when practicing it.

You need to be love spending much of your time on your computer since most of the swing trading markets are online platforms. You need to be excited when trading. This will motivate you to learn more about it and you will get much informed. Knowledge is powerful since it leads to success.

Do your trading with all the passion and enjoy it. You can also join forums with swing traders' experts to learn and see what others are doing. Swing trading is not an easy thing, you need to have much love and passion for it to succeed. A bored swing trader gets tired with time and decides to give up with trading. Be the happy trader and success will definitely come your way.

✔ Come up with Good Swing Trading Decisions.

The kind of decisions you make in trading defines you a lot. Do you expect success when you come up with poor decisions? A swing trader needs to make strong and good decisions while trading. You need to prepare yourself so well mentally on the best thing to do when the different market situations occur.

Do not be the kind of trader who makes poor and rushing decisions when things fall apart. Be a good decision-maker for better success in the future. Also, do not rely so much on what people are saying online. You need to come up with your own decisions for your own trading. Others may mislead you and this might make you fail terribly. Be strong and do the right thing.

The Swing Trader Mindset

Beginners are prone to making mistakes in any endeavor. The problem with the stock market is making mistakes can be extremely costly when you are a trader, even leading to bankruptcy. Nevertheless, by learning from the mistakes of others, you can avoid falling prey to the biggest problems that might come your way as a result of your inexperience.

Failing to exit a losing trade

It can't be said enough; all too often people let emotions take over their judgment in the stock market. When you set up a big swing trade, you might get overconfident and excessively excited about it if you are new to the business. Moreover, if the stock starts moving the wrong way, you might hold onto the trade when you should simply exit and take your losses. Sometimes people can't believe it when a "sure thing" turns out to be a loss, and they hold on too long hoping things are going to turn around. Waiting too long can be costly —sometimes catastrophically so. We hate to beat a dead horse – but protect every trade you make with stop-loss orders rather than letting emotion take over.

Exiting Too Soon

The right time to exit a trade can be a difficult thing to figure out. That's why it's best to plan ahead of time and set an exit point where you are going to be comfortable with profits.

If you go into a swing trade without a definite plan, it's going to be too easy to fall prey to a situation where you might get out too soon, afraid that you aren't going to be able to make any profit and fearing possible losses. You can also get fooled by temporary downturns. Remember that there are always counter trends on the way up. Don't be fooled by the counter trends into exiting too early. Emotion can get heavy immediately after placing a big trade. Also, remember that you should set a time frame for your trade to work out. Swing traders are not day traders, so don't get the impulse to exit a trade two hours after you've entered the position.

Believing shares won't lose value

Unbelievably, some people have the same attitude about stocks that people used to have about housing, which is that stocks won't decline. Sometimes they do, and they don't recover. Just because it's Google or Apple, it doesn't mean that losses aren't possible.

Too much margin

Swing traders can actually access a lot of margins. That means that you can borrow to buy shares from the broker. That can be a problem if you end up losing big, you might end up owing the broker a large amount of money. You need to be extremely careful with margin, and all things considered, it is better to grow slowly by making methodical trades with money you already have than it is to borrow lots of money in hope of quickly growing your account.

Waiting too long for price declines

There are ideal price points to buy shares. However, you shouldn't always wait to reach a level of support before buying. Sometimes a stock might be entering an upward trend, and it's going to establish a new level of support. If you wait too long hoping the price is going to drop down to the last level of support, you might miss out on the opportunity.

Believing past performance is a guarantee of future performance

This is one of the biggest fallacies of the stock market. You cannot take the past performance of a company's stock as an ironclad guarantee that the stock is going to perform the same way going forward. Past performance indicates little compared to the company's current fundamentals, trading volume, volatility, and the trends and indicators for the stock in the here and now. Just because Amazon grew a lot in the past five years, it doesn't mean it will continue to do so.

Investing more than you can afford to lose

It's easy to get excited about the amount of money you can make swing trading, and it's also easy to get excited over all the charts, all the action, and the thrills of making winning trades. This can lead some people into pulling out too much money from savings and retirement accounts to enter into larger trades. That is a big mistake. You should always keep in mind that you need to set up trades where you can afford to lose it all, so your personal savings, college savings accounts, and retirement accounts won't be impacted, and you won't have trouble paying for your basic living expenses. Set aside the excitement and prepare for a long journey where you grow your business slowly, so you don't end up in the poor house.

Get started with small and achievable profit goals, and when your trades go bad as some inevitably will, your losses will be minimal.

Now we'll look at the swing trader mindset. This will be a mix of characteristics and attitudes you should have before even becoming a swing trader, and also a set of behaviors and mindsets you should adopt once you become a swing trader.

You must be Risk Tolerant

Most investors have a low tolerance for risk. That is why they put money in savings accounts and mutual funds. Becoming a swing trader can be said to put you in an elite community. That isn't to say that swing traders are better people. What we mean by this is that swing trader are a small group relative to the overall population. The vast majority of people are not willing to risk their capital in order to realize large, short-term gains. While a swing trader is more cautious (and some would say more rational) than a day trader, compared to the average outlook that most people have if you are interested in swing trading that indicates a much higher tolerance of risk.

You are not ruled by emotion

A successful swing trader is not going to be someone who is ruled by emotion. You are going to enter into and exit your trades based on a cold, hard examination of the facts.

Someone who is caught up in emotion when stocks start moving up fast or sliding down is not someone who is suitable to be a swing trader.

Emotional decisions can lead to many bad trades and can even be catastrophic. The average person can panic when a certain trend appears in the stock market. There is no room for panic if you decide to become a trader, keeping a cool head at all times is essential.

You do your homework

A swing trader is not going to trade based on their gut. That is something amateurs do. Of course, we always hear the winning stories, but most of the time people trading on their gut are going to lose out. As a successful swing trader, you should be trading based on a thorough background check of the situation. You should be doing your homework by picking 2-3 of your favorite technical analysis tools, studying candlesticks and trends, and also studying the fundamentals of the company and keeping up with financial news. Only after you've thoroughly evaluated a stock should you consider entering into a trade. People who don't do their homework might win some of the time, but at the end of a year when you compile all the wins and losses, people that don't do their homework are going to finish last unless they got very lucky. The world isn't governed by luck unless you're at a gambling casino. Despite the unfair reputation, trading might have among the ignorant public, swing trading is not gambling, and so isn't governed by luck.

You are disciplined

A swing trader is disciplined. This really follows on the heels of the previous point, but a swing trader is someone that studies everything carefully and takes the time to study all of the technical analysis indicators and trends they are going to use in their analysis. Then you will have the discipline to develop a trading plan, and you're going to have the discipline to stick to the trading plan. When becoming a swing trader, whether you're going to do it full-time or only on a part-time basis keeping your day job, you need to look at swing trading as a business. You wouldn't run a business based on temporary emotional outbursts. If you did, you could easily end up broke. For example, suppose you find some kind of craft made in China and open a shop to sell them. The third day your shop is open; someone comes in and praises them and buys three. You get super excited. Do you then take your entire life savings and buy 1,000 more? We hope not.

Swing trading needs to be approached in the same way. View it as a business and make a business plan that you are going to follow. You are not going to get rattled by missing out on potential gains in the share price. For one thing, until any gains happen, they are nothing but imaginary. It is better to sell when you can do so and take a profit. Second, you are not in this to make a large profit off one trade. Of course, if you have a great trade, all the more power to you. However, generally speaking, swing trading is about earning money steadily from trades over the long term and slowly growing your business. It is not a get rich quick scheme, so don't think of it that way. If you can make a $1,000 profit from a trade, you are doing quite well, and you can reinvest the money to continue to grow your business with time. Any time you are making profits from a trade, it is going to be a time to be happy, even if it is only $100.

Amateurs are the ones who are going to fret because they "missed out." More often than not, share prices are going to drop off from some peak if you hold on too long, and you will miss out on what you could have had if only you had the discipline to sell at the right time. That is more dangerous than missing out on some "big thing" that could have netted you huge returns.

You prepare for all outcomes

As part of running your swing trading as a business, a good swing trader prepares for all outcomes. That is why we included the one order cancels another approach in this book. Everyone expects profits, but they don't always materialize. Therefore, you need to be as prepared for losses - in fact, more so – as well as being prepared to cash in profits. Preparing for all outcomes means first determining the risk level you are willing to accept for your account. You have to set a risk level you are comfortable with, the 1-2% level is recommended by market experts, but that doesn't mean you have to follow it exactly. However, no matter what you do need to set a level of risk so that if you did lose the capital, you are not going to be hurt financially. Of course, any loss of capital hurts, but you shouldn't be having to go into debt or begging on the street corner to make your house payment because you made a bad trade. You also need to make sure that not only are your losses not catastrophic, but if you do take a loss, you still have enough money to enter into another trade.

Also, be aware of creeping losses. If you keep losing $500 per trade without making any gains, you need to take a look at your trading practices and dial back your level of risk. A $500 loss one time is one thing, a $500 loss every week can add up fast.

You can adjust your strategy

Emotion can take over in many ways when trading. Money has that effect on people. One way that emotion can overtake you is if you develop your own system for swing trading, and you start making multiple winning trades. Then something in the market might change, and maybe you start losing lots of money. In that case, are you going to be beholden to your old system, or adjust to the changing conditions? A successful trader is going to be one who makes the adjustments. Don't take it personally, when things stop working. Always fall back on doing the analysis, remember that hard facts rule the day at all times, not your love of Apple, Netflix, or even your own trading methods.

You might also take a look at what indicators you are using. Maybe it's time to try different indicators. On the other hand, maybe you are even relying on indicators too much, or putting too much stock in trends.

Successful traders don't stop learning

This book should be taken as your first step. A successful trader is one who is open to continuous education. There are always things to learn from others that can help make you a better trader. You should be putting in an effort to educate yourself to grow your knowledge about finance, the stock market, and business.

That includes watching YouTube videos, taking courses, and reading as many books about the subject as you can. You should also watch plenty of financial news so you can learn about current conditions and how people think they are going to change. They aren't always going to be right, but the more knowledge you have, the better positioned you are going to be when it comes to being a successful trader.

Don't give in to euphoria or despair

We are all going to have big winning trades and massive losses at one point or another if we trade for any length of time. Whether you experience a big loss or not is not the question, it's how you react to it. Persistence and objective analysis about what went wrong with the trade are the proper ways to respond. Falling into emotional despair is unproductive and doesn't help the situation. First off, if you give in to emotional despair, you are not going to learn from your mistakes. You are also letting your emotions take over and take control of your actions. Of course, if you have followed the principles outlined in this book, you won't have any catastrophic losses – but if you do then review the principles behind managing risk, dust yourself off and try again.

Euphoria over a big winning trade can be as damaging. Book your winning trades and be happy about them, but don't let yourself be overcome by mania.

Also, don't waste money.

Sure, you can take a little out to celebrate, but again, you should treat this as a business and reinvest most of your profits. Long-term growth of your business should be the number one goal. If you are living off your trades, only take out what you need to take out. Don't blow a winning trade on a new car and a trip to Europe. It's also important because it might lead you into entering into a lot of bad trades in the aftermath. Sometimes people can get overconfident and then blow themselves out of the water because they let their euphoria take over and they overtraded.

Swing Trading Strategies

You've probably been reading this book and wondering at what point we will start to talk about swing trading strategies. After all, you are probably most interested in the actual strategies that you can apply to make money swing trading. You can see though, that there is a lot to learn before you can start to understand the strategies that people use to swing trade. The market has many factors at play, and you need to understand the tools used to assess companies and their technical movements. You won't be able to use the same strategy in every situation, so knowing how to read the market is the first step before learning strategy.

The indicators that you are looking for will depend on the type of strategy you are using, so pay close attention to the fundamental characteristics of companies and you'll start to recognize similarities amongst different opportunities.

The first step is to make a habit of mining for opportunities. There are a lot of fascinating economic and business journals available on the internet that you can peruse for information about current events and finance news.

You never know how you will identify your next opportunity. An article about energy companies in Texas may inspire you to research energy contracts in the American Southwest, and which companies to watch for.

An article in a tech news magazine might send you on a hunt for publicly traded companies developing a certain type of computer hardware. If it intrigues you, then let yourself be drawn in for further research. The important thing is to spend a little time each day reading and identifying possible opportunities. Once you've noticed an opportunity, dig a little deeper and review the company's involved and check out their fundamentals. How have these companies been performing? Is it worth taking a position?

You can do this research by looking at the market sector by sector. Find indexes that represent different sectors you are interested in and check up with them every day. It's good to have a relatively broad field of interests from which you can identify options. One sector might be ripe with opportunities while another sector lags on the same day. Being able to switch gears and focus on the place where opportunities are happening will make you a more effective and well-rounded trader.

The type of strategy you use will also affect what characteristics you'll be looking for. If you are willing to take on a little more risk and you want to try swing trading, then you will be looking for stocks that show signs of a moving downwards. With the uptick rule, you will have to find stocks that are moving up now, but you have reason to believe that they will continue to drop in the future.

If you want to buy a stock and hang on to it and make a profit, then you'll be looking for stocks or sectors that are healthy and have continued and consistent growth.

The earlier you enter a position, the better.

Look out for signs of reversals as both a short seller and a bull trader. The sooner you enter a position after a true reversal, the more you can earn.

Remember the tenet of Dow Theory that states that the average of all the stocks in the index should confirm each other. You may just take a position on one or two stocks, but its good to have a picture of the entire sector. This will tell you whether you will be swimming upstream or downstream. It's OK to swim upstream as long as you feel like you have a compelling reason.

When you have identified a stock that balances risk and reward ratio, decide what price you'd like to buy-in. This will require some research into the fundamentals of a company so you can evaluate whether you are overpaying or underpaying.

One strategy that you can employ as a swing trader is known as gap trading. A gap is when there is a significant difference between the closing price of a stock today, and the opening price of that stock tomorrow. As a swing trader, you can try and take advantage of these gaps by anticipating that gap and choosing a favorable position. There are instances when the gap could go against you; like with a secondary offering or a bad financial report. But there are just as many instances when you can try to predict a gap.

Swing traders have an advantage over day traders because they can use this gap.

Day traders are also less susceptible to the risk that the gap creates.

Depending on your outlook and your strategy, you may see the gap as either a good thing or a bad thing. Unfortunately, with gap trading, you don't have much control if the stock price moves against your position. You just must wait for the market to open the next day in order to react.

Gaps could open in several ways. A company could release a statement of earnings, and as a result, the price of the stock could drop or go up significantly in a short amount of time. Unfortunately, it's hard to anticipate a company's earnings report in order to make an educated guess on a good position. Most investors consider it to be too risky to play the gap on an earnings report because it's too easy for there to be a surprise when the company releases its statement.

Another way to take advantage of a gap is by researching companies that are developing new technologies. This type of stock can be very volatile, with attitudes changing swiftly about the predicted success or failure of the product. The volatility could be an opportunity for the swing trader if they timed it right. Just be aware of the way the market can respond to an announcement about new technology. The stock price may shoot up to unprecedented levels as a result but often, things will settle down shortly after. Knowing how to time a position during a product announcement will be a major factor in whether you stand to make any money.

Remember; not all products succeed either. Sometimes a new product can hurt the company, in the long run, more than it helps them in the short run. Imagine an automotive company that announces the release of a new model. For a while, the model could increase anticipated earnings and investors might flock to the company. But the first model of the car might have more issues than expected, and the safety rating may be lower than normal. Remember that Dow Theory says that every action results in a reaction on the market. A product that performs poorly can do just as much harm as a product that performs well. Keep track of the progress of the companies in your portfolio, and make sure you time your positions well.

Another way a swing trader can ride a trend is to seek industries that are experiencing booms. Look for industries that are 'trendy'. Right now, the marijuana industry is experiencing a major boom and investors who recognized the possibilities of this trend early are enjoying a growing portfolio. With the legalization of Marijuana in Canada and many states in the US, there are new companies popping up all over as demand for the product is growing. Eventually, there could be a bubble once the expansion adjusts. But trends like these present opportunities for swing traders. Whether or not you decide to invest in the marijuana industry, its an example of a rideable trend. Who knows how it could play out?

These opportunities that exist in trends don't come around too often, and a swing trader must be patient in order to identify them.

Usually, though, all one needs to do to find out about these trends is read the newspaper. Trends come and go and the window for making a real profit is limited. But if you're patient then there will always be another trend around the corner. The trick is to keep your ears to the wind so that you know when an opportunity has arrived.

Just like any swing trading strategy, a lot of it comes down to timing. A good example of a famous trend is the dotcom bubble in the 90s and early 2000s. A lot of people made big off the rise in internet technologies and computer companies. Eventually, though, the trend took a major dip and there were just as many losers from the dot-com trend as there were winners. Just remember that the stock market works in cycles and patterns, and these patterns often repeat themselves. Monitor your positions and stay up to date on news cycles.

When it comes to deciding on a position, timing is important. This means not only timing your exit but also timing your entry. It's better to be patient and wait for a good opportunity to buy when the stock price is low than to try and rush in out of impatience.

Before you open a position decide how much you are willing to pay. This is important because when you have a target price you can calculate exactly what you are risking before you even take on a position.

Again, it's better to figure this out before you even take the position.

Once you've determined an entry point then you must be patient.

Wait for the price of the stock to match your ideal price. If it doesn't, then move on. Never forget that being a good trader requires discipline, which includes knowing when you should take an opportunity and when you should look at other options.

There are ways to track the price or set entry points without the need to constantly monitor the market. For example, a lot of brokerages offer alert services where you can receive notifications when the price of a stock has reached a predetermined target. You decide on an entry point and go about your day, then you receive a notification from your broker. You can even give them a limit order, which tells your broker to buy the stock for you once it hits that target. These notifications are also available for sale targets, so your broker can let you know when the stock has reached that target. They can even sell it automatically for you.

You've read about setting an exit point by now, and how sometimes you'd like to leave some flexibility in case the stock price continues to move in your favor. One way to do this is by not exiting your position all at once. Let's say you a buy a stock and the price of that stock has risen beyond your exit point and it is still moving. You want to preserve some of your earnings, but you are also curious about how high the stock might go. You take to exit your position with only a portion of your money while leaving the rest in. You slowly withdraw your position in increments, but you maintain some percentage of your position until you are completely ready to withdraw. This technique is called scaling out.

Intermediate and Advanced Trading Strategies

Throughout this guidebook, we have spent some time taking a look at some of the different things that you can do when it comes to trading with swing trading. Now, it is time to take it a bit deeper and look at some of the more intermediate and advanced trading strategies that you can use. As you progress with your swing trading, get a better idea of how it works, and are ready to take it a bit further to see what results you can get, these strategies are going to be the best options for you. Some of the different advanced trading strategies that you can use with swing trading include the following.

Moving Average Trend Trading

The first strategy that we are going to take a look at here is the moving average trend strategy. This moving average is important because it is going to be the way that you can pick out when you want to enter and when you want to exit a trade for a specific stock. There are many stocks that are going to start out the morning doing well in the morning trend, and they will have a strong upside or downside trend. You would then watch their charts and see where the moving averages go in the charts. This is beneficial to the traders because you will then be able to follow the moving average to figure out which trend is occurring and you can ride out that kind of trend.

While this strategy does sound like it takes a bit of time to figure out and it may seem complicated to work with, it is pretty easy to learn how to use properly.

Some of the steps that are needed to make this one work for your needs include:

• When you take a look at the graphs that you want to use and you are checking out the stock you want to use, make sure that you look to see whether or not a trend is forming near the spot that is the moving average. When you do see this, you will want to get into the market and use this strategy. You can then spend a bit of time looking at the trading data that shows up for that stock from the day before. This is important to see how the moving average changes and how the stock is going to respond to that average.

• After looking over the charts and getting a chance to see which moving average is the best one for the trade you are doing, it is time to make a purchase of the stock. Some traders do choose to wait a little bit longer in order to confirm the moving average before they enter. But, either way, try to purchase as close to the lines for the moving average as you can.

• Once you are ready, you need to pick out the stop points that you want to use. You may want to consider setting the stop just a bit below the moving average line to help protect your investment, but it still allows for a little bit of volatility of movement.

If you are doing this strategy with a candlestick chart, then you need to make sure that you have a start that is close to the moving average and choose to work with a long position.

• After you have these in place and have been able to enter the market, you can just ride on that trend until you see the moving average break and then take your profits.

For this kind of strategy, it is important to remember that you never want to work with a trailing stop on this strategy. This one is also a strategy where you need to pay full attention to the market or more than usual because there are times when the market can end up getting away from you.

While the scanner can be great for helping you get the right trades, you need to make sure that you use your own eyes rather than the scanner when you are ready to use this kind of strategy.

If you see that your chosen stock is moving really high from the moving average, this means that you are making a great profit. At this time, it may be best to take the half position rather than going all the way to your break. This is going to make sure that you make some profit, and sometimes, you will see the moving trend go down before the break. If you let this happen, it is possible to lose out on all of the profit. But, with the half position, you can at least make some profit.

Resistance Trading

The next option that we are going to take a look at when it comes to trading is the resistance trading strategy.

Support and resistance trading are also very popular when it comes to doing swing trading; you will probably find a lot of traders who choose to work with this method instead of one of the others. The support is going to be the price level when buying is really strong, so strong that it can interrupt or reverse the current downtrend that may show up in the charts.

When your current downtrend gets to a support level, it is going to bounce back at least a little. When you are looking at your graphs, this support line is going to be shown on a chart with a horizontal line that needs to connect together at least two bottoms together.

Then, we have to take a look at the resistance, which is going to be the opposite. This will end up being the price level where you see a strong selling position, one that is so strong that it can reverse the uptrend that is going on in the charts. When you see the uptrend hit this level, the trend is going to stop, and sometimes, it will go down. The resistance is going to be represented similar to the support, but it will connect together two or more tops.

In some cases, it is possible to get a minor resistance or a minor support. These are going to cause a little pause in the trend. But, when you work with the major support or resistance, it is going to be able to force the trend to reverse. Traders who are working with this kind of strategy will try to make a purchase as close to the support as possible, and then, they will sell as close to the resistance as possible. This helps them to get the most out of each trade.

In order to figure out these support and resistance levels, you need to take some time to look at the daily charts of your chosen stocks. Sometimes, this line is even hard to find, and you may have to wait a few days in order to find a clear line that you are comfortable using. This means that patience is needed with this kind of strategy as you may have to wait a bit to get started with this strategy at all.

There are some steps that you can use the charts that you have available to help draw your own support and resistant lines. Some of the steps you can take to make this process easier and to really use this **strategy include:**

• Remember those indecision candles? You are going to see these in areas of support and resistance. These candles often show that buyers and sellers are fighting with each other to see who has the most control over the price.

• Often, half dollars and whole dollars can be good support and resistance levels. This is especially true when you work on stocks under $10. If you can't find your support or your resistance lines, check here and see if your line would work there.

• When you make your own lines, you need to have the most recent data available. This ensures that you are getting the best information for that stock.

• The more that your line is able to touch the extreme price of the stock, the better option this line is for your support and resistance. If it is too far from this extreme point, then it is not going to have enough value to make it strong.

- Only look at any support or resistance lines that stay with the current price range. For example, if the stock's price is around $20 right now, you do not need to look at the region on the graph where the stock randomly jumped up to $40. This is not an area where the stock will probably go back to, so it doesn't make much sense to work from there.

- Many times, the support and resistance is not just one exact number. Often, it is more of an area. If you come up with a support or resistance that is about $19.69, then you know that the movement is somewhere near that number and not exactly that number. You can usually estimate that the area is going to be somewhere between five to ten cents above or under that line.

- The price that you want to work from will need to have a clear bounce off that level. If you can't find that this price bounces at that level, then this is not a good support or resistance level for you to work with. Your levels need to be really easy to notice and need to make sense for the charts you look at. If you have any questions about whether you picked the right one or not, it's not the right one.

When you go onto the charts and create these lines, you may find that drawing the perfect line can be a challenge. You need to make sure that you are picking out the right lines for the support and for the resistance so that you know how to base the trades. But, the best way to ensure that you are doing this the proper way is to take the time to practice. Over time, you will get better, and this will be a great strategy to go with.

Opening Range Breakout

The next strategy that we are going to take a look at when it comes to advanced strategies for swing trading is known as the opening range breakout. This strategy is a great one to work with because it provides you with a good signal for when to enter the market, but it does make it more difficult to know where you should target the profit. You have to go through and do some of the work on your own, and you can pick out the profit that you would like this trade to reach based on some of the other strategies that we have discussed. The opening range breakout is often one that a trader is going to use if they need a good signal for entry, but you will then need to come up with the right exit point for your trades as well.

To work with this kind of strategy, you need to pay a lot of attention to what shows up in the market. When you are taking a look at some of the stock charts at this time, you may see that the Stocks in Play are going to have some violent price action. Buyers and sellers are going to flood the market during the first five to ten minutes when the market opens. This can be a very crazy time to trade. New investors are often going to stay out of the market during this time because it is too volatile for them to see results.

But, there are some investors who are going to take a look at this market opening and decide that their position did go down during the night. There are some who will panic because they don't realize what is going on at this time, and they will try to sell their stocks and hopefully make something.

There are also a lot of new investors who will come to the market at this time, see that the stock is being offered at a discount from the panicked seller, and will purchase the stock at that great deal. Both of these movements are going to be important because they are going to help you determine the price of the stock, and it gives you a good idea of what is going to happen during that day.

As a swing trader, it is important to wait out that first little bit of the market. It is often best to wait at least the first fifteen minutes or so before entering the market. This ensures that you don't get stuck in the market and run into trouble along the way as well. You want to wait until after all the craziness has had some time to pass before you try to join the market and end up getting in on the wrong side of a position.

Like with many of the other setups that we have talked about in this guidebook, the opening range breakout strategy is going to work the best with either mid-cap or large stocks or ones that won't go through huge and unpredictable price swings while you hold onto them.

You also want to make sure that you don't go into this type of strategy with some low float stocks. Pick out a stock that has the ability to trade inside a range smaller than the ATR or the Average True Range.

When working with the opening range breakout strategy, there are a few steps that you will need to follow.

These steps include:

•   After you have had some time to create your watchlist in the morning, you should wait until the stock market has had time to settle down, so wait about five minutes. During this time, watch the price action and the opening range. You can also check out how many shares are traded during that time and then figure out from that information if the stock is going down or up. This time is when a ton of orders go through the market and you want to look at these numbers to see how liquid a stock actually is.

•   During this time, you can also look through to see what the ATR of that stock is. You want the opening range to be smaller compared to the ATR so make sure that the ATR number is nearby.

•   Once those first five minutes of market opening are finished, you may see that the stock will stay in that opening range a bit longer depending on what traders and investors want to do. However, if you see at this time that the stock is breaking out of this range, it is time to enter the trade. Enter the trade going the same direction of the breakout. If you can, go long if you see the breakout is going up, but go short if the breakout is going down.

•   Pick out a good target for your profit as well. You can find this by looking at the daily levels from the previous day and identify where the stock is before the market opens. You can also look at the previous days' close, along with the moving averages, to come up with a good target.

- If you can't find the right technical level for your chosen target or for the exit, you can choose to go long and then look for signs of weakness. On the other hand, if you want to take a short position and then the stock goes high, this shows you the stock is strong, and you want to cover the position as much as you can.

You will want to work with this method whether you want to work with a shorter or a longer time frame. But, the steps above are done with a shorter trade of just one day. You can go in and expand it out to fit the needs that you have when it comes to swing trading.

.

Trend

Okay, we've looked at stages and waves. Now let's turn our attention to trends.

To put it simply, a trend is the relatively consistent price movement in one predominant direction within a particular time frame. These price movements could be either sideways, up, or down so long as they are fairly consistent for a considerable amount of time. Trends may last for as long as several months; a huge profit-making period for traders who can see the bigger picture.

Countertrends

It is possible to have a countertrend within a predominant trend (the bigger picture). This is not just a pullback or a rally; it is period where a trend goes in the opposite direction of a major trend for as long as several weeks or months. However, its price movements eventually return to the major trend. This is good for you as a swing trader because you are not in the market for the long-haul. So you can make a profit from both the predominant trend (bigger picture) and from the countertrend.

Short-term Trends

Within the predominant trend, there is also the possibility of having short-term trends which are super cool for swing traders.

Short-term trends can sometimes last for as long as several days to weeks.

But guess what: short-term trends are usually not apparent when you are looking at the bigger picture – the predominant trend. You need to zoom in closer to see them. So, take a look at any stock chart that shows a predominant trend for several months, but this time, magnify the chart to show you daily trends. You can zoom in closer to see hourly or shorter time periods. There you will find swing trading honeypots that are of no interest to the buy-and-hold investor, but which are goldmines to the swing trader!

Trending Stocks

As a beginner, if you really want to make money from swing trading over and over again, you should trade trending stocks (stocks that are in an uptrend or downtrend). And here is how to know a trending stock. A stock in an uptrend has higher highs and higher lows. In other words, a stock in the second stage is in an upward trend. Also, a stock in a downtrend has lower highs and lower lows. That is to say; fourth stage stocks are in a downward trend.

Generally, stocks are either in a trending phase or they are in a trading ranges phase. It has been roughly estimated that stocks are in the trending phase for about 30 percent of the time. The rest of the time, they are in the trading ranges phase.

Now take a good look at another chart below to see if, as a beginner, you would prefer to trade during a trending ranges phase.

Ignorance is what makes people who are new to swing trading enter trades during the trading ranges phase.

It is very risky because there is hardly a chance of predicting any trend up or down. Trading ranges usually occur during the first and third stages of a stock movement. Remember, we said that you should stay in cash (hold 'em) during these stages. One of the fastest ways to throw away your capital is to trade stocks when they are in the trading ranges phase.

A Note about "Buying Cheap"

When stocks are falling excessively (in a critical downtrend), a swing trader may be tempted to go long excessively (buy larger amounts of stock) because falling price means cheap stocks. I would recommend that you should be very careful when attempting to buy into such stocks. If you must buy, you should utilize stop orders. Let me briefly explain why.

You see, in the stock market, as well as with every other aspect of life, "cheap stocks" usually have a tendency of eventually becoming cheaper. It may not happen all of the time, but it does happen. However, there is a possibility of cheaper stocks to rebound. But it may take a long time for cheaper stocks to bounce back up; time which a swing trader does not have. In other words, if a swing trader rushes into "buying cheap" he or she may end up amassing cheap stocks that no one will be interested in buying back. I believe that is not your aim for venturing into swing trading, yes?

Bottom Line

Practice looking at charts and pinpointing whether they are in the trending or trade ranges phase.

It is a huge mistake to go long or buy a stock that is heading in a downtrend simply because you notice a sudden upward price movement. If the stock is truly in a downtrend, then the sudden upward price movement is a rally that doesn't last. It usually quickly returns downward, and that is a great time to go short (sell). The opposite applies to an uptrend. Do not go short because you observe a pullback. It usually bounces back in a short while.

The sudden downward price movement is an excellent time to go long (buy stocks) before the bounce back happens.

Conclusion

Traditionally swing trading continues to be described as a speculative technique as the roles are usually purchased as well as held for the trader's fixed timeframe. These time frames could vary between 2 days to a couple of months. The objective of the swing trader is usually to determine the trend either up or maybe place and down the trades of theirs is probably the most advantageous position. From there the trader is going to ride the pattern to what they decide when the exhaustion point in addition to sell for an income. In many cases swing traders are going to utilize a variety of technical indicators that will enable them to have a far more advantageous probability when making the trades of theirs. Shorter-term traders don't always usually swing trade as they choose to hold positions during the day and working out them before the close of the marketplace. Swing trading tactic utilizes time and it's this time which will be the deterrent factor for most day traders. In many cases there's way too much risk associated with the close of the marketplace and that a trader won't be happy to accept this risk.

The distinction of swing trading is an extensive subject in its numerous various influences from a wide range of various trading methods. Every one of these trading techniques are unique and also have the respective risk profiles of theirs.

Swing trading is usually a great way for a market place participant to further improve the technical analysis skills of theirs while offering them a chance to pay a lot more focus on the essential side of trading.

Several effective swing traders have been recognized to utilize a Bollinger band program as a tool to help them in entering as well as exiting positions. Naturally, for a swing trader to achieve success in the technique, they are going to need to get an impressive aptitude for identifying the present industry trend and putting the positions of theirs in accordance with that pattern. It does a swing trader note great to put a brief position with the program of holding for a prolonged time period of a market place which is certainly trending upwards. The general theme here's the aim of the traders must be increasing the probability of theirs of success while limiting or even eliminating risk completely. The swing trader's most detrimental enemy is the fact that associated with sideways or in the market that is active. Sideways price actions are going to stop a swing trader cold in his or maybe the tracks of her as there's absolutely no prevailing pattern to key out of.

When utilized properly swing trading is a superb approach used by lots of traders across various different market segments. It's not just applied to the Forex market though it's a vital instrument of equity and futures markets. Swing traders take the abilities they discover through technical analysis and may also parlay these skills into different options strategies.

The short term dynamics of swing trading sets it apart from which of the standard investor. Investors generally have a longer term time horizon and aren't usually impacted by short-term price fluctuations.

Of course, one must keep in mind that swing trading is just one strategy and must be utilized just when appropriately understood.

Like every trading strategies swing trading is able to be conservative and risky strategies can become day trading strategies rather quick. In case you plan to use a swing trading program, make sure that you completely grasp the risks and create a method that will have the opportunity to enable you to produce optimum portion returns on the positions of yours.

Swing trading is 1 of trading types which generally implemented in speculative activity in monetary markets like bonds, foreign exchange, commodity, stock as well as inventory index. Generally this trading design takes a swing trader to keep his or maybe her trading job over one trading day, often two to five trading days. Swing trading is common in the trading community as this particular trading types normally have an excellent reward and risk ratio, it indicates the probability to increase profit is bigger compared to the chance that could increase in each trade.

Generally, swing trading aims for a hundred pips earnings probability. Benefit potential could be acquired from every industry swing. A swing trader, particularly for international exchange as well as stock index sector, can go both short or long to take every chance. Additionally, it means, inside a trading week, when a market place is volatile, a swing trader can come across many trading potentials he or maybe she is able to capture.

CPSIA information can be obtained
at www.ICGtesting.com
Printed in the USA
LVHW052124120121
676284LV00002BA/33